Political parties and pressure-groups in Britain

Political parties and pressure-groups in Britain

Geoffrey K. Roberts

Lecturer in Political Science
University of Technology, Loughborough

St. Martin's Press   **New York**

JN
1121
.R62
1971

Copyright © by Geoffrey K. Roberts
All rights reserved. For information, write:
St. Martin's Press, Inc., 175 Fifth Avenue, New York, N.Y. 10010
Printed in Great Britain
Library of Congress Catalog Card Number: 73–175009
First published in the United States of America in 1971

AFFILIATED PUBLISHERS: Macmillan & Company, Limited, London – also at Bombay, Calcutta, Madras and Melbourne – The Macmillan Company of Canada, Limited, Toronto

Dedicated to the memory of
Sigfrid Henry Steinberg
(1899–1969)
mentor and friend

Contents

	Introduction	ix
1	Groups and politics	1
2	British political parties: *a*. history	13
3	British political parties: *b*. functions and organization	29
4	British political parties: *c*. leaders and followers	50
5	Pressure-groups	78
6	Groups and policy	108
7	Constraints	131
8	Groups and the political system: comparison and contrast	153
9	Conclusion: the plural society	176
	Further reading	195
	Index	199

Introduction

This book attempts to introduce to the reader the somewhat involved, and very important, subject of political parties and pressure-groups, those influential organizations which do so much to shape the decisions which the more formal of our political institutions make for us – Parliament, the Cabinet, the ministerial and local government departments. These decisions alter our lives almost from day to day, in the form of new taxes, restrictions on various activities such as motoring, foreign travel, or bank loans, new obligations in such fields as industrial safety, town planning, or the organization of public transport, new commitments to overseas allies or international organizations – the list is endless. And involved in many stages of the making of these decisions are groups: political parties, interests, lobbies, and pressure-groups.

Inevitably, in one book no writer can hope to cover comprehensively even the more obvious aspects of these groups. But the topics which are examined in this book are, it is assumed, of interest and of importance: the history, organization, functions and leadership of these groups, and how they operate within the context of the British political system. For further reading, a selection of other works of a more specialized nature is given after the concluding chapter.

My obligation to the advice and scholarship of Bernard Crick, my former tutor at the London School of Economics, and now an editor of this series, is most gladly acknowledged, as is my gratitude to my wife, Mechthild, for her assistance with the typing and preparation of the manuscript for publication.

G.K.R.

1 Groups and politics

'US' AND 'THEM'

Ask people in Britain today if they think that they, as individuals, have any influence on the way in which they are governed, in influencing the policies – national or local – decided upon in their name, and they will frequently reply: 'How can I have any effect on them?' or, 'What can one person do among 35 million?', or, 'The Government makes all the decisions.' Yet, despite these widespread feelings of individual powerlessness, it is true that about three-quarters of the electorate, for one reason or another, will turn out to vote at a general election. This may be from loyalty to a party or from dislike of one of the candidates, from a sense of civic duty, or family pressure, or just as a gesture of support or opposition to the record of the government of the day. It is probably just as true that, between elections, at least as many will exercise the ancient British privilege of grumbling about the government, whether they voted for it or against it. But the tax demands arrive, the costs of electricity, gas, public transport or house mortgages increase, schools go comprehensive, rates increase, valleys are flooded, villages are expanded into towns for overspill population, unemployment increases, wages are 'frozen', speed limits are imposed, and so on, and so on, without the 'man in the street' imagining that he has any say at all in these important decisions.

Why, then is it still asserted – by prime ministers, the 'British Constitution' text-books, the candidates on the hustings, the radio overseas broadcasts, for example – that, in Britain, not just the policies of the government but also its very existence depend upon popular acceptance and support? Why cannot the present administration simply declare that it will stay in power for the next decade, instead of testing its popularity at a general election not later than five years after the last one was held? To make things even more complicated, in what ways can it be said that the policies of the government do depend on popular support? Take any one of a number of recent controversial policies: Rhodesia, support for American action in Viet-Nam, steel nationalization, the ban on pirate radio broadcasting, the application to join the Common Market, the Anglo-French 'Concorde' project, the abolition of the death penalty for murder. Probably everyone disagrees with the adoption of at least one of these policies. Some would like stronger action over Rhodesia, others recognition of its independent status; some would have preferred that less compensation had been paid to the former owners of the steel companies that were nationalized, others would have liked steel to remain in private ownership, and so on. The evidence of the opinion polls suggests that, on some of these issues, a majority of the electorate (perhaps even a majority of Labour voters at the 1966 election) would vote against the particular policy adopted. Yet, because there is no provision for a referendum on individual policies in the British system of government, the victorious party lays claim to a mandate for its entire electoral programme, by virtue of being returned to Parliament with a majority of seats. It is in this sense that British governments rely on popular support for their existence.

It is plain that the opinions and the vote of one ordinary elector among 35 millions will usually not have much effect on a policy or a government. Even in a constituency of between 30,000 and 100,000 electors, it will probably not be decisive. Along with other votes, though, sometimes only a small number of others, it can be important. In the 1966 election, the result at Peterborough was only declared after the votes had been counted eight times, and the margin of Conservative victory was just three votes in a total of 52,000. Even in what may appear to be a safe seat, if a number of people are over-confident that their party will win without their vote, or feel that the weather is too bad to make the effort of voting, a surprise like Brighton Kemptown (where a Conservative majority of over 5,000 became a Labour majority of seven votes in 1964) or Carmarthen (a Labour majority of 9,000 in 1966 was turned into a Welsh Nationalist majority of 2,436 at a by-election only four months later) can easily occur. In the American Presidential election of 1960, in which over 68 million people voted, if 4,500 voters in Illinois and 28,000 in Texas had voted Republican rather than Democratic, they would have given their states to Nixon instead of Kennedy, and with them the Presidency. In the British general election of 1964, if a total of 350 Labour voters had stayed at home in four constituencies (Brighton Kemptown, Wellingborough, King's Lynn and Colne Valley) Labour would not have had a clear majority in that Parliament.

Nor is it only the effect of votes at a general election that is important. Local elections and by-elections, while not necessarily deciding which party acts as the government, can serve as warnings or as encouragement to the government regarding the general course of its policies. Before the Second World War, the St George's (Westminster) by-election in 1931 signalled the victory of Baldwin as Conservative leader over the criticisms of his policies and leadership by the Press Lords (Beaverbrook and Rothermere in particular), and the East Fulham by-election of 1933 was taken (certainly by Baldwin, the Prime Minister) as a sign of growing support for disarmament and pacifism. The unexpected Liberal victory in the Orpington by-election in 1962 was followed by large-scale changes in the Macmillan Cabinet, in addition to acting as a stimulus to the Liberal Party. The 1967 local and by-election results, following so soon after the triumph of the Labour Government at the 1966 general election, indicated the dangers to their popularity among the voters caused by the austere economic policy, and the controversial educational changes they had pressed forward.

Generally, though, in spite of these rather exceptional cases of election surprises, members of the public feel powerless, or at least irrelevant, in the face of the highly-organized structures of government. The vote at a general election may be high, but it is less likely to be high at by-elections,[1] while at local elections it often falls to one-third or one-quarter of the qualified electorate. The viewing figures for election broadcasts by party leaders may be high, perhaps largely on account of such broadcasts being given peak viewing time between

[1] In between the elections of 1959 and 1964, in only two by-elections: Montgomery, and Kinross and West Perthshire, did the turnout exceed either the preceding or the succeeding general election percentages; in the other sixty it was lower than both general elections. In the period 1964–66, none of the thirteen by-elections matched either of the general elections for turnout.

popular programmes, but the degree of knowledge concerning politicians or policies exhibited by the public through opinion polls, etc., is very small.

A 'GOLDEN AGE'?

Faced with a situation of declining individual interest in politics and influence on politics, some observers might be tempted to look back to the previous century, when Victorian individualism and civic pride, coupled with ideas of the proper limitations of spheres of government concern, meant that political life was both less complex and more responsive to the wishes of the citizens. To many other countries, especially within the Empire, the British political style provoked both envy and imitation.

Certainly at first glance there seem to have been significant differences between then and now. Even after the Reform Act of 1832, eight parliamentary constituencies cast fewer than 200 votes at the 1832 general election, and many had majorities of less than 100, making the 'weight' of each vote of considerable significance. The large, highly organized groups that inhabit the corridors of power in order to put pressure on government or Parliament today were almost completely unknown then.[1] Political parties, which sometimes appear to monopolize political business nowadays, were more like family groups or clubs of metropolitan gentlemen, than the mass-organizations we know today. But of course this is neither an accurate nor a particularly helpful contrast, for many reasons. First of all, the population was much smaller 150 years ago,

	Population of the United Kingdom		Percentage of the population over 21 eligible to vote
1831	17,835,000	1800	3
1851	22,259,000	1832	5
1901	38,237,000	1867	13
1951	50,225,000	1884	25
1965	54,436,000	1918	75
		1928	100

[2] See below, Chapter 5.

and in addition the proportion of that smaller population who could, in any meaningful sense of the term, be called the political public, was also smaller.

The social similarities that existed between members of the Government, Members of Parliament, local leaders, leaders of industry, landowners, the cultural figures of the period, and the smaller electorate were much stronger than exist today.[3] The problems of government were confined broadly to the fields of internal and external security, problems of colonial administration, overseas trade, taxation and religious questions. Only occasionally did Parliament bother itself with unusual questions such as slavery, parliamentary reform, industrial relations or industrial development. Contrast the restricted range of subjects debated in Parliament in any Hansard of the early nineteenth century with the multiplicity of issues that may be raised in question-time, debate or committee in any week in Parliament in 1969: agricultural subsidies, broadcasting, foreign affairs in a world of over 100 states, transport, control of education, location of industry, reform of the legal system, the complications of defence policy or the public control of areas of development hardly imaginable then, atomic energy, rail and air transport, electricity.

As the scope of governmental business has increased, so have two other important dimensions of political life: communications and organization. Both of these processes have significant effects upon the relationship between popular opinion and government action. New methods of communication have been developed which enable government to be carried on at a much swifter pace than was ever possible in the past. Try to imagine for a moment the problems a government would face today if it were unable to make use of typewriters or copying machines, telephones, the radio or television, speedy transportation by road, rail and air, and with only a primitive postal service, a narrowly circulated press, and requiring frequent contact with a generally illiterate population. Take these methods of communication away from the parties, and how could they participate nationally at a general election, with an electorate of 35 million? Take them

[3] See below, Chapter 4, for a discussion of contemporary social characteristics of leaders and followers in political parties.

away from pressure-groups, and how could they conduct a national campaign, or preserve a national membership, or communicate their views effectively to the politicians? These advances in communication are still not fully exploited, of course; the campaign for the introduction of television cameras into Parliament, if successful, would be another method of improving communications between 'us' and 'them', whatever its other advantages or disadvantages.

Communication facilitates organization, and the complexity of political organization has kept pace with these new developments. The size of the cabinet, the number of departments and ministers, the strength of the civil service establishment, the sophisticated bureaucracies at the party Headquarters in Smith Square, the armies of officials in town and county halls, the multitude of public relations staff and similar employees in the headquarters of pressure-groups – these indicate unequivocally the complicated configuration of the contemporary 'map of power'. Even a politically alert citizen, with ample time and material resources available, would find it very difficult to discover who was responsible for a particular decision, how he could attempt to get it changed, or even the grounds for the decision in the first place. Perhaps, in some ways, politics was simpler in 1800.

PARTIES AND PRESSURE-GROUPS

As measured by the proportion of the adult population who have the right to vote for Members of Parliament (and, in doing so, to choose the Government for the next few years), or by the lip-service paid by political parties to 'government in the interests of the whole community', Britain has attained the status of a democracy over the past century and a half. Yet each citizen as an individual may well feel that he has less political power, less influence on the shaping and direction of public affairs, than was possessed by his nineteenth-century counterpart. The corollary could well be that 'they' – the politicians, especially the leaders of the Government and the Opposition, but also public officials – have become more powerful than ever. Even the powers of the people's representatives, the Members of Parliament, are seen as being dangerously in decline; it was the early nineteenth century, not the twentieth, that has been called 'the golden age of the private Member'.[4]

The vital qualification to such a pessimistic outlook for democracy can be found in the existence, and, much more, in the power of political groups which filter and focus the multiplicity of demands that the citizens have on government, which take up informed positions on the important issues of the day, and which in return can provide support for a government which attempts to satisfy some of these demands. Just imagine the chaos there would be in a complex, highly-populated society like Britain if everyone tried to communicate his demands or opinions directly to the government. Filtering and abridgement would still have to be carried out, probably by a vastly enlarged civil service, before the Minister could make sense of the multitude of opinions offered. This would hardly be more democratic, or more efficient! Without parties and other groups, how would the priorities of public demand be satisfied? How could the government attempt to collate such demands, or categorize them, or choose between conflicting demands? This can perhaps be done directly in a family, in a parish council, at a tribal meeting or in a trade union branch, but for a 'mass society' other means than the direct gathering of opinions must be found. Only in elections (or referenda in other countries) is such a direct method used, and the direct costs of organization, polling and counting the results, as well as the hidden costs of the disruption of 'normal activities' are discouragingly large.

For the sake of convenience, it is necessary now to categorize political groups into two sets: political parties, and pressure-groups, and although some parts of this book will still consider these in general terms, their purposes are sufficiently distinct to deal with separately.

Political parties have as their major purpose success through the electoral system with a view to forming the Government, and, at a local level, controlling the local council and its major committees. Such success is not, of course, required for its own sake, nor for the prestige or patronage that accompanies it in

[4] R. Pares, *King George* III *and the Politicians* (Oxford University Press, 1959), p. 192.

Britain. It is the legitimate means of implementing a wide-ranging programme of political policies, which in turn may be said to reflect a more or less explicit set of values or 'ideology'. There are all kinds of other functions carried out by political parties in Britain, some consciously, others almost accidentally: political education, acting as a means of social mobility, research leading to the development of new policies, the provision of recreational activities, and so on. But unless it has some hopes, however meagre, of putting a programme into practice, a group cannot properly be termed a 'political party'.

Pressure-groups, sometimes also called 'lobbies' (an American term) or 'interest-groups', are organized to influence policy in a relatively limited number of areas, sometimes, indeed, only in one area, such as commercial broadcasting, agriculture, the abolition or retention of the death penalty, ex-servicemen's pensions, motoring, or our relations with a particular foreign country. They attempt to exert this influence over the government or Parliament or local authorities, but they do not themselves seek to act as the government. This distinguishes them from political parties, and it is sometimes a difficult, though necessary, distinction to make. What of the political parties which – barring catastrophe of some sort, or some great political upheaval – will never in the foreseeable future play a direct part in the government of Britain? In this group come the Communists, the Nationalist Parties of Wales, Scotland and Northern Ireland, and probably even the Liberal Party (though its members would be quick to disagree). What of the groups which, despite the strictly limited nature of their policy, occasionally put up a candidate in an election: the Unilateral Disarmament Campaign (Twickenham 1964) or the Anti-Common-Market groups (Dorset South 1962)? When does a group become a party? The Labour Party in this country was formed precisely for a particular and limited purpose: to obtain a greater voice in Parliament for representatives of the interests of the working man[5]; in other countries military,

---

[5] The resolution of the TUC in 1899 read:
'This Congress, having regard to its decisions in former years, and with a view to securing a better representation of the interests of Labour in the House of Commons, hereby instructs the Parliamentary Committee to invite the co-operation of all the Co-operatives, Socialistic, Trade Unions, and other

religious, and ethnic groups have sought to win elections to press for their particular interests – the Catholic parties in Europe in the nineteenth century, pro-military candidates in Japan before the Second World War, the Polish Party in the German Second Empire.

Finally, while considering classification of political groups, the existence of pressure-groups *within* political parties should not be overlooked. They may exist to press for a particular type of strategy, or to promote a special policy. Recent examples in Britain are: the Campaign for Democratic Socialism, which sought to reverse the decision of the Labour Party Conference at Scarborough in 1960 which made unilateral nuclear disarmament official party policy (the decision was in fact reversed at the Blackpool Conference the following year), PEST ('Pressure for Economic and Social Toryism') which hopes to bring the Conservative Party up-to-date, and the Monday Club, which tries to maintain what it chooses to regard as the basic principles of Conservatism. But, however they are classified, they all act as influences on decisions taken by Parliament and the government.

DEMOCRACY AND POLITICAL GROUPS

In the last analysis, the political power that is possessed by the leading politicians in any country, be it democratic, autocratic, totalitarian or feudal, derives from their position in relation to certain political groups. Such groups may be political parties – especially in a one-party state – or important interest-groups based, for example, on industry, on ethnic divisions, or even on support from a powerful neighbouring country. They may be religious; consider the power of the Catholic Church in the states of medieval Europe. Or the group may be quite simply the organized expression of coercive power: the police,

working organizations to jointly co-operate on lines mutually agreed upon, in convening a special congress of representatives from such of the above-mentioned organizations as may be willing to take part, to devise ways and means for securing the return of an increased number of labour members to the next parliament.'
(P. Poirier, *The Advent of the Labour Party* (Allen and Unwin, 1958), p. 74, quoting the TUC Annual 1899, pp. 64–65.)

or, more usually, the military. If the support given by one group declines, it may be possible to replace it by support from another group. One explanation for the turmoil in China is that the leaders are struggling to retain or win over the support of important groups: the Army, students, the peasantry. One of the most significant features of nineteenth-century British politics was the way in which the Tory leadership became increasingly aware of the need to gain the support of the urban lower-income groups to compensate for the relative decline in importance of its traditional rural upper-class strength, particularly after the extension of the franchise in 1867. Its success in such a strategy is demonstrated by its long possession of office up to 1906. Some influential Liberals today wish their party to appeal to sections of the electorate usually considered to be Labour inclined, to replace its former middle-class support.

From these examples, it is clear that not all such group support for the leaders in power is 'organized' in any formal sense. What is present, though, in all these groups, is a sense of common identification with an ideology, or programme, or even with an extremely vague set of values, for example of a class nature. Such values will be communicated to the leadership, which will ignore them at its peril. It may not be able to satisfy all of the wishes of the group, and in any event there may be more than one group to satisfy, whose demands may conflict. But enough must be done to convince these groups that their interests would probably not be better served by switching their support to other leaders.

One of the distinguishing features of a democratic political system, compared to an autocratic or totalitarian system, is the method by which such changes of government can come about. In the latter cases, extremely powerful pressure, or even revolution, will be the only possibilities, since the system itself will not allow for change by any other means. In democracies, however, periodic opportunities to change the leadership will be available. In Britain, for instance, this takes the form of a general election, for which, with very minor exceptions, all British adults may register as voters, and such elections must be held at least every five years. In the United States, the legislature and the President are elected separately, at fixed intervals, but again (in theory) the right to participate in such a change is given to the citizenry at large. In both these instances, and in practically all the other states that we would care to label democratic, an increasingly important role is taken in elections by political parties, at all levels of society, and an increasingly influential part is assumed by pressure-groups and interests, whether the unions, the farmers, the Negro or Jewish or Welsh Nationalist voters, the middle-classes, the tax-payers, the commuters or even vaguer categories such as the youth vote.

This connection between groups and democracy involves certain implications for the leadership of the political system. Much has been said and written in recent years about the increasing 'power of the Prime Minister' in Britain, and the dominance of such party leaders as Churchill, Macmillan and Wilson vis-à-vis their colleagues in the Government would seem to bear out such a statement. But however powerful a Prime Minister might seem, however much he may appear to dominate his colleagues, he must be most careful to preserve sufficient support among his fellow ministers to retain the leadership,[6] sufficient support from the party in Parliament to forward his programme, and, if at all possible, sufficient support among the electorate to retain power at the next election.

So we return to the point made earlier, that in a nation, if not in a small group, democratic choice in politics implies the existence of groups, generally in the form of political parties, to make such choice meaningful. The groups themselves, whether political parties or not, may arise through a number of different circumstances: different attitudes to wealth and property, different religious beliefs, different interests or specialisms, particularly of an economic nature, geographical divisions, and so forth. These differences are the very basis of

[6] Although the party leader is elected in all three parties by the votes of the MPs, unless there is a credible alternative among the leading MPs, he will not be opposed, and unless such an alternative can feel some confidence in carrying other leading members of the party with him in the event of victory, he will not want to stand. The challenge to Attlee in 1945. which failed because Ernest Bevin refused to support it, and the complicated manœuvres that surrounded Home's succession to the leadership of the Conservative Party in 1963 both took account of this.

politics – the existence of a variety of possible answers to political problems, the recognition that it is probable that no one set of answers will hold for all problems, in all circumstances, at all times. The vehicles for such politics, the proponents of these differences, are political groups. Since, in Britain, the major groups representing such choices are the political parties, the next three chapters will examine the ways in which these groups came into existence, how they are organized, how they work in practice, and the relationships between their leaders and their supporters.

2 British political parties:
a. history

There are three ways of studying British political parties. The conventional way is to begin, as with any organization, with a plan of its various units and branches: the leadership, the national representative organizations, the professional staff, the constituencies, the youth groups, and so on – as it were, an anatomy of parties, similar to that set out in Fig. 1 (pp. 36–7). To persevere with the biological analogy, clearly such a study on its own would appear somewhat lifeless, revealing little of the part played by parties in the political process.

A second way of proceeding would be with a 'physiology' of parties, an analysis of their formal and their more informal functions: selecting candidates for office, campaigning at election time, choosing leaders or evolving new policies. This would prove a more exciting study, and would account for much more of the actual behaviour of political parties, but of course from time to time it would still be necessary to answer questions about the restrictions on possible types of party activity by referring to its 'constitution' (whether written or unwritten), or its pattern of organization, or its official procedures.

When the further questions are considered of *why* such and such a rule, or arrangement, or procedure was adopted in the first place, or *why* changes might be difficult to implement, we are brought back to the third, and perhaps the most logical, of the methods of studying political parties: the historical approach. For this approach has the advantage of constantly reminding us of the inter-relationship between organization, behaviour, and the events of history itself. It helps to explain why the Labour Party spent so long in the 1950s and the early 1960s arguing over 'Clause IV' or defence policy, how the Conservatives recovered so quickly from the landslide defeat of 1945, or what brought about the rapid decline of the once-great Liberal Party, which before the First World War governed with one of the most talented administrations of the century.

This chapter will therefore describe briefly how the British party system developed, the part played by political parties in the transition from the aristocratic government of the eighteenth century to 'mass democracy' in our own times and the way in which traditional struggles of Tories and Whigs, Conservatives and Liberals, were replaced by the more fundamental class-based conflict between Conservative and Labour parties. The examination in the next chapter of what parties do in contemporary politics, and the ways in which they are organized to carry out these functions, should then be easier to comprehend.

THE EVOLUTION OF PARTIES BEFORE 1832

In the 'pre-history'[1] of political parties the word 'party' was used to indicate a variety of groupings, sometimes over religious questions, at other times referring to the sides in a dynastic dispute or a constitutional quarrel. In any case, until the reign of the Stuarts, politics was a matter of king, ministers, and Parliament rather than anything that remotely resembled the political parties of a later period. Royal authority was still very real indeed, and it was only when the very basis of this authority was called into question, leading to the Civil War between Royalists and Parliamentarians that broke out in 1642, that the divisions were created that gave rise to the modern party system.

Following the Restoration of Charles II, the Royalists in Parliament tended to divide among themselves over the policies pursued by the government. Such division reached a crisis in 1679, over an attempt by the House of Commons to exclude James, Duke of York, from the succession to the throne (on the grounds that he was a Roman Catholic) and led to the formation of the Whig and Tory parties, uncomplimentary nicknames that denoted the opposing groups on this question of the 'Exclusion Crisis'.

[1] The term is used in I. Bulmer-Thomas, *The Growth of the British Party System*, vol. 1 (John Barker, 1965).

Factions indeed were at this time extremely animated against each other. The very names, by which each party denominated its antagonist, discover the virulence and rancour which prevailed. For besides petitioner and abhorrer, appellations which were soon forgotten, this year[2] is remarkable for being the epoch of the well-known epithets of WHIG and TORY, by which and sometimes without any material difference, this island has been so long divided. The court party reproached their antagonists with their affinity to the fanatical conventiclers of Scotland, who were known by the name of Whigs; the country party found a resemblance between the courtiers and the popish banditti in Ireland, to whom the appellation of Tory was affixed.[3]

From these groups can be traced the Liberal and Conservative parties of our own period, though in some places the line of descent is very blurred indeed.

Though passions ran high at the time of the Exclusion Crisis, the abdication of James II and the so-called 'Glorious Revolution' of 1688 which, under limitations, gave the throne to William of Orange (William III), modified the party struggle in several ways. First, it became less fashionable or profitable to call oneself a Tory after the triumph of the Whigs, and particularly after the crown passed to the Hanoverians after the death of Anne. To be Tory was to brand oneself as a malcontent, a sympathizer for the lost cause of the Stuarts. Second, the temptations of office led many ambitious politicians to abandon party labels, or to call themselves 'Whigs' irrespective of their real political opinions, and this furthered divisions within the Whig Party itself. Third, there was still in Parliament, as well as outside it, a large proportion of politicians who were either genuinely independent of party, or were supporters of the Monarch, regardless of which party provided the government. Fourth, religious and other issues came increasingly to complicate the seemingly simple questions of the extent of the constitutional powers of the King and Parliament. Certainly party labels gave no guarantee of coherent policy from either the Government or the opposition.

One authority[4] has said of the political divisions of the

[2] 1680.
[3] David Hume, *History of Great Britain*, vol. II (London, 1824), p. 532.
[4] K. Feiling, *The Second Tory Party* (Macmillan, 1938), p.v.

eighteenth century that, though there was no party system, there was 'a continuous tradition and some elementary framework of party, and a descent of political ideas'. Though developments occurred in the reigns of Anne, the four Georges and William IV, that can be seen as contributing to the evolution of a two-party system, they were intertwined with a whole series of constitutional developments involving the political role of the Monarch, the power of Parliament (Lords as much as Commons), the invention of Cabinet government, and the gradual emergence of the office of Prime Minister. The whole tangled narrative suggests an atmosphere of tremendous potentiality. British political institutions in the eighteenth century were robust, and were capable, as Burke put it, of 'reforming in order to preserve'. One cannot imagine that, like the French institutions of the time, they might have suffered destruction at the hands of exasperated revolutionaries,[5] but almost anything else might have been possible. There could have been a measure of parliamentary reform fifty years ahead of its actual time (a start was made in the 1780s, but the French Revolution intervened), the partial resumption of monarchical powers in abeyance since 1688 (and certainly George III tested parliamentary and popular resistance to such resumption on several occasions), a strengthening of government by the 'squires and shires', or their supplantment by a new industrial aristocracy, bringing the enterprise of commerce into the business of state. In none of these possibilities, nor in the metropolitan based oligarchic rule that actually continued up to 1832, was it in any way predestined that political parties should have a role, and certainly not that they should provide the instrument through which the policies of state would find implementation.

The parties of the eighteenth century were far removed in every respect from the highly organized national institutions of today. Less than half the members of either House could be labelled Whig or Tory in any case. Those that could be classified in this way belonged to a multitude of small groups,

[5] Nor is the fate of the American colonies a parallel case; what is noteworthy is the degree of continuity of American political institutions before, and after, the war of independence: a property franchise, the office of Governor, two-chamber legislatures, etc.

bound to their leaders to a varying extent by loyalty, family, patronage or interest, but rarely by simple principle, far less by support for a specific programme agreed upon in advance, despite Burke's famous eighteenth-century definition of party as 'a body of men united, for promoting by their joint endeavours the national interest, upon some particular principle in which they are all agreed'. These groups might federate to form a government, but, like many federations of political organizations, they lacked sanctions or rewards other than those that could be obtained through mutual co-operation. 'Court' and 'Country', 'Government' and 'Opposition' (often scorned as near-treasonable faction in those days), could be just as important categories of political action as Whig or Tory.

George III disliked parties, for they provided centres of loyalty for groups, which he could not then control. Many leading politicians also had little liking for organized party structure, for this might interfere with their own powers, and dilute the efficiency of patronage which magnates such as the Duke of Newcastle could use to provide themselves with a personal following. Organization was confined in Parliament to elementary whipping-in of known supporters on an issue, the social gatherings at the great political houses or the clubs, and, in the constituencies, when a contest did occur, some cursory canvassing.

Towards the end of the eighteenth century, ideas of 'responsible' government were being put forward, whereby a government which lost the confidence of the Commons gave way to one that could obtain such support. This encouraged the organization of party groupings ready to assume office in such circumstances. There still existed a 'party of the Crown' (i.e. those peers and MPs who, through patronage, contributions from the salaries of government officials they had nominated to lucrative posts, particularly in the Customs and Excise services, and other inducements, were reliable supporters of the king's position irrespective of the policies of the government of the time). But it was declining in numbers and influence, which increased the proportion of members of both Houses ready to assume party loyalties. Rudimentary constituency organization could be found in a few areas. One of these was Westminster, under the leadership of Francis Place between 1807 and 1820, where skilful organization enabled the Radicals to counter Tory influence.

By the early nineteenth century, then, the two-party system was becoming more apparent. The Whig rhetoric spoke of 'reform, Parliament and the people', though within their own ranks they were divided on the definitions and implications of these terms. To a Wilkes, 'the people' could encompass the mobs of the City; to a patrician like Grey it was a much less inclusive term, linked to respectability, property and economic independence. This combination of Radicalism and the Whig aristocracy gave birth to the reforming, middle-class-based Liberal Party of Gladstone in the second half of the century.[6] The Tories were for 'King, Church and Constitution', but the variety of interpretations they gave these causes was illustrated by their divisions over Catholic Emancipation and parliamentary reform. Many of these party divisions were based on personal followings; Creevey, a diarist of the period, noted in 1810 that there were some five distinct groups within the Tory Party.[7]

Organization was still primitive and sporadic. Finance for party purposes was obtained as required from the personal wealth of the leaders, and from private donations, generally on the announcement of an election. The party whose leaders were in power could also count on the Secret Service and similar official funds. In both Houses a rudimentary Whip's Office was created for each party. But the history of parties, in the style we know them today, really begins with the passing of the 1832 Reform Act.

THE NINETEENTH CENTURY: THE MATURING OF THE PARTY SYSTEM

'The modern party system is of course a direct product of the expansion of the electorate.'[8] The two best known features of the

[6] On the Victorian Liberal Party, see D. Southgate, *The Passing of the Whigs* (Macmillan, 1962), and J. Vincent, *The Formation of the Liberal Party* (Constable, 1966).

[7] I. Jennings, *Party Politics*, vol. II (Cambridge University Press, 1961), p. 69.

[8] R. McKenzie, *British Political Parties* (Heinemann, 1955), p. 6.

1832 Reform Act are its expansion of the electorate, particularly by its creation of a uniform borough franchise, and its redistribution of parliamentary seats from the rotten boroughs to the new industrial cities. The third feature, and one which was of even greater importance to the development of the modern party system, was the requirement in the Act of the registration of voters in advance of an election. Constituencies were in many cases still small enough for a handful of votes to make the difference between victory and defeat. Of course, the traditional electoral practices of bribery and intimidation in various forms continued to be employed, but their effectiveness could also be increased by constituency organization. The new dimension of registration now meant that a local organization, active in the period between electoral campaigns, could succeed in removing known opposition voters from the register (the secret ballot was still forty years away) and at the same time could pack the register with the names of more of its own supporters. Since methods of appeal against the inclusion or removal of a voter's name were complicated and costly, the parties were in the best position to handle claims and objections, and the local party agent developed into an important political figure. From registration duties, his activities extended to the organization of canvassing, the hiring of committee rooms (usually public houses) and the tactics of keeping back voters until the closing stages of the poll (which spread over several days) so that an over-confident opponent would not have time to whip-in sufficient additional support to win.

Some of these practices had been known in pre-Reform elections, as Charles Dickens, in *The Pickwick Papers*, described the Eatanswill election, and the tactics of Mr Perker, the agent of one of the candidates, Samuel Slumkey:

'You have come down here to see an election – eh?'
Mr Pickwick replied in the affirmative.
'Spirited contest, my dear sir,' said the little man.
'I am delighted to hear it,' said Mr Pickwick, rubbing his hands. 'I like sturdy patriotism, on whatever side it is called forth – and so it's a spirited contest?'
'Oh yes,' said the little man, 'very much so indeed. We have opened all the public houses in the place, and left our adversary

nothing but the beer-shops – masterly stroke of policy that, my dear sir, eh?' – and the little man smiled complacently, and took a large pinch of snuff.

'And what are the probabilities as to the result of the contest?' inquired Mr Pickwick.

'Why doubtful, my dear sir; rather doubtful as yet,' replied the little man. 'Fizkin's people have got three-and-thirty voters in the lock-up coach-house at the White Hart.'

'In the coach-house!' said Mr Pickwick, considerably astonished by this second stroke of policy.

'They keep 'em locked up there till they want 'em,' resumed the little man. 'The effect of that is, you see, to prevent our getting at them; and even if we could, it would be of no use, for they keep them very drunk on purpose. Smart fellow, Fizkin's agent – very smart fellow indeed.' . . .

A small body of electors remained unpolled on the very last day. They were calculating and reflective persons, who had not yet been convinced by the arguments of either party, although they had had frequent conferences with each. One hour before the close of the poll, Mr Perker solicited the honour of a private interview with these intelligent, these noble, these patriotic men. It was granted. His arguments were brief, but satisfactory. They went in a body to the poll; and when they returned, the honourable Samuel Slumkey, of Slumkey Hall, was returned also.

No candidate could be confident of a seat until he had secured the approval and co-operation of the local agent. The result of such activity was appreciated in 1841, which was the first case of a government going into a general election with a majority and being replaced by an opposition which was disciplined and organized for electoral purposes.

Such an improvement in local organization was matched by refinements of parliamentary organization. In 1835 the Tories had a committee working on the organization of the election, suggesting candidates, using influence, and offering some financial support to certain candidates. More attention was paid to the need for a party Leader who could command the support of the whole party, rather than merely act as the leader of a powerful personal clique. Party meetings, previously held infrequently for the purpose of announcing policy decisions, came to be held more often, and were occasionally used to consider the merits of alternative courses of action. Such seemed to be the case with the Conservatives' 1867 Reform Bill:

Derby and Disraeli took the then unusual step of summoning a party meeting on the 15th and expounding the Bill to their supporters before presenting it to the House three days later. Derby declared that he would recommend a dissolution if beaten on any major issue – a threat that did much to keep the waverers from wavering. The innovation of a party meeting was a great success. It made members feel that they were being kept in the picture, that their advice was appreciated and that their leaders trusted them. If Peel had pursued the same course over the Corn Laws he might have fared better.[9]

When Bills were introduced more care was taken over backbench opinion than was previously the case, for the penalties for rebellion by a party supporter were still hardly more serious than being passed over for office. The organization of the Whip's office was improved, especially by Peel's skilful party manager, Bonham, and the Chief Whip took increasing responsibility for election management. The practice of party leaders in opposition meeting together gave rise to a type of shadow cabinet, ready to form an alternative government when the opportunity occurred. The greater difficulty experienced in obtaining illicit funds from the sale of seats or the use of government monies meant that more attention had to be given to securing finance from other sources. Much care was taken with the press, in order to present the best party case, and to answer the propaganda of the other party.

There was no extra-parliamentary national representative organization until after the 1867 Reform Act, but in the intervening period the 'political club' acted as a centre and co-ordinating body for the party. Such clubs 'combined the functions of central office and national party conference.'[10] The two leading clubs, set up primarily for political rather than social purposes, were the Carlton and the Reform, for Tories and Whigs respectively. Membership included the parliamentary party and others of influence in the party, for example party dignitaries from the provinces. The club was the centre of party information, the collecting point for party subscriptions,

[9] R. Blake, *Disraeli* (Eyre and Spottiswoode, 1966), p. 463.
[10] N. Gash, *Politics in the Age of Peel* (Longmans, 1953), p. 394.

the home of electoral committees, and the place where aspiring candidates could hope to be put in touch with suitable constituencies. The new-style party manager or 'general agent' would be found here, particularly near to election time, and his endorsement came to be equivalent to official party recognition for a candidate.

The national party organizations were the result of a desire to co-ordinate efforts in the constituencies, and a need to improve election prospects in a period when the parliamentary parties were coming to see elections – and the results – much more on a national scale. The Liberal Registration Association was set up in 1860 to co-ordinate the constituency registration associations, and, more especially, to establish committees in poorly organized seats where Liberal victories could be hoped for when organization was improved. The 'minority clause' of the 1867 Act [11] led to the highly-efficient organization of the Birmingham Association to get round this restriction, and thus elect a full slate of Liberal candidates. This powerful electoral machine was imitated – not always successfully – in other towns, and in 1877 a conference of local associations was called in Birmingham to form a National Liberal Federation.

In the Conservative Party, the National Union of Conservative Associations was set up in 1867, and in 1883 an unsuccessful attempt was made to give it a more influential, if not a controlling, role within the party. This was frustrated by the party leadership, who saw no advantage in diminishing the degree of central direction in the party. The establishment of nine provincial unions did not occur until 1886.

Thus the situation at the close of the nineteenth century was as follows: the changes in electoral politics (especially the enlargement of the electorate, the secret ballot, registration, and the virtual elimination of corruption by legislation) had forced the parties, in order to attract votes, to adopt more sophisticated methods, including the creation of local and national organizations outside Parliament. They also had to pay greater attention to campaigning and raising money before elections took place. But the parliamentary party, under parliamentary leadership as provided by Gladstone, Disraeli,

[11] Under this clause, in multi-member seats returning more than two MPs, the voter had one fewer vote than the number of seats to be filled.

Salisbury or Rosebery, was still supreme, and did not necessarily feel itself bound by any suggestions or directions from local or national party organs. This did not prevent such organizations from discussing policy – the Newcastle Programme[12] which influenced Liberal policy from 1891 is an example – but their position was still very much auxiliary to the party in Parliament.

The cumulative effects of these changes had meant that politics became much more influenced by the middle- and skilled working-classes, even though their strength at the polls was hardly reflected in their representation in the Commons. The House of Commons itself was still aristocratic in connection, and the activists of the working-class for this reason decided to attempt to establish their influence in Parliament itself.

THE LABOUR PARTY

The Labour Party began outside Parliament, unlike the Liberal and Conservative parties. In fact, it was many years before its parliamentary party reached the state of supremacy over its national organs that the other parties enjoyed, though, however much the rank-and-file and party activists may resent it, and despite the strictures of the Party Constitution, such supremacy is well-established today.

The reforms of 1867 offered great opportunities for working-class organization. In 1869 a Labour Representation League was created to promote the election of Members of Parliament favourable to Labour, though this group declined after a few years. The Social Democratic Federation was formed in 1881, and the Independent Labour Party in 1893. Yet these, and similar groups, were not very successful in gaining parliamentary recognition. By no means the whole of the working-class yet had the vote, money was short and political experience was lacking. Co-operation with the Liberal Party seemed to offer more possibilities. A number of Liberal-Labour candidates were elected, and a few even promoted to minor office (such

[12] A series of radical policies adopted by the Party Conference which met at Newcastle in 1891, and accepted by Gladstone as the basis of the Liberal platform.

as Henry Broadhurst, Gladstone's under-secretary at the Home Office in 1886), but these were insufficient, either to affect the direction of the Liberal Party, or to satisfy the growing political ambitions of Labour.

In 1889 the Trades Union Congress carried a resolution [13] which demanded a conference of trade unions, co-operative and socialist groups, in order to plan for greater labour representation in the House of Commons. This conference met in 1900 in London, and it agreed to set up a Labour Representation Committee, financed by subscriptions from affiliated organizations. This was a modest beginning to what later became a great enterprise, especially as many unions, from which the bulk of the subscriptions and affiliations were expected, showed little enthusiasm in the beginning.

By good fortune, as much as by organization, two of the fifteen candidates endorsed by the Committee – Bell and Keir Hardie – were elected at the 1900 general election, and this, together with the Taff Vale decision[14] in 1901, boosted membership considerably. Subscriptions were increased in order to pay Labour MPs a salary. Payment of this salary in turn had the effect of increasing the control of the Committee over the MPs.

By 1903 Labour was sufficiently important for the Liberal Chief Whip to make a secret electoral pact with them through Ramsay MacDonald (who was to become Labour's first Prime Minister). To avoid dividing the anti-Conservative vote, in certain constituencies Labour would stand down in favour of the Liberal candidate, and in return in other constituencies Labour would be allowed a clear run. In some double-member constituencies, one candidate from each party would stand. This arrangement went into operation in 1906. Thanks to the Liberals' exaggerated estimates of Labour strength and to MacDonald's skilled bargaining, of the fifty candidates who stood, only eighteen faced Liberal opposition. Twenty-nine of these fifty were elected, to add extra strength to the massive Liberal majority. This was a vital breakthrough for Labour. On the assembly of Parliament, the first major

---

[13] See above, p. 8, for its wording.

[14] A judgment of the House of Lords which allowed companies suffering financial loss in strikes to seek damages from the trade unions involved

action of these MPs was to assume the new title of 'Labour Party'.

THE TWENTIETH CENTURY: 'MASS PARTIES' AND 'MASS SOCIETY'

The transition from small, leader-based parliamentary parties, with varying, but never overwhelming, degrees of power in the political system, to large organization – based national parties which can claim with some truth to be the most powerful, and indeed the decisive, elements in British politics was completed in the twentieth century. Many of the factors which caused this transition existed in the nineteenth century, and some, such as the expansion of the electorate, and the secret ballot, have already been mentioned. Others were only really important in more recent times, though they may have roots in the nineteenth century.

Among these are the collection of social and cultural institutions which became 'national' rather than local or provincial in this century. Communications are an obvious case: the decline of the provincial press, the general concentration of ownership of newspapers, the development of radio and then television, the improvement of telegraphic communication, the nationalization of rail and air transport, all contributed to a London-based cultural homogeneity in social and political life that in the nineteenth century would have been challenged by the Manchester of Cobden or the Birmingham of Chamberlain. Collectivization as a political development,[15] not solely due to the influence of the Labour Party, can also be seen to have had consequences for the party system: state control of the social services and education, regulation of important areas of the economy, interference with miscellaneous matters ranging from the location of industry to the marketing of eggs and potatoes, for instance, all affected the style and focus of party competition. The overwhelming preponderance of national politics over local issues (witness any parliamentary candidate's

[15] 'In short, what kinds of organization groups would adopt, what modes of political action they would follow and what ends they would pursue, were dependent upon the legitimating ideas of Collectivist politics.' S. Beer, *Modern British Politics* (Faber, 1965), p. 389.

election address) and the parallel national organization of the major interests in the state, required that any party with pretensions to govern should produce national policies and possess national organization.

Changes in the political system itself were also influential. The Lloyd George coalition in 1918 may not have provided 'homes for heroes to live in', but it did ensure that the heroes – and heroines over the age of 30 – could now vote for their parliamentary representatives, which increased the total electorate quite substantially. Women were put on an equal electoral footing with men in 1928 (when they were given the so-called 'flapper vote'). The payment of Members of Parliament commenced in 1912, and this not only permitted candidates without independent means or a second profession to enter Parliament, but increased their dependence on party approval for the continuance or advancement of their parliamentary careers. The gradual elimination of independent Members, and the reduction in Liberal representation to a mere handful, forced governments to treat any major defeat in the Commons as a vote of no confidence, which in turn made strict party discipline imperative.

The Labour Party, despite the encouragement of its 1906 successes and its ability to secure favourable legislation from the government as the price of its support, made little headway in the elections before 1918 (73 seats) and 1922 (142 seats), when it was able to profit from the wider franchise and the war-time division of the Liberal Party. It developed the organization of constituency parties, whereas previously it had only sponsored candidates adopted locally by trade unions, affiliated groups, etc.; it improved its parliamentary and national organization; and in 1918 it adopted a revised Constitution. This Constitution, besides providing for individual membership of local constituency parties, and the representation of these local parties at the Conference, reformed the organization of the National Executive (incidentally increasing the power of the trade unions on the composition of the NEC), and gave a clear statement of the Party's objectives: 'To secure for the producers by hand or by brain the full fruits of their industry, and the most equitable distribution thereof that may be possible, upon the basis of the common ownership of the means of production and the best obtainable system of popular administration and control of each industry and service.'

This Clause IV thus tried to attract a wider range of support to the party, and at the same time committed it to a socialist platform, even if the word socialism itself was avoided. The power of the Leader and the parliamentary party was given considerable impetus by the formation of the two minority Labour administrations of 1924 and 1929. The 'betrayal' of the party by Ramsay MacDonald in 1931 (by joining a Conservative-dominated coalition which opposed non-coalition Labour candidates at the 1931 election) led to a reaction in favour of extra-parliamentary control. But the dominance of Attlee as Prime Minister from 1945–51 ensured that the Labour Party, at least in office, was directed by its Leader and his foremost colleagues, and resolutions by Conference, though influential, would not be considered binding if they were embarrassing to the parliamentary leadership. In any event their implementation was recognized to be a matter of Cabinet priorities.

The importance of the post-1918 period to the *Conservative Party* was that at long last 'Tory democracy' became a phrase that could have some application to the party itself. The choice of Baldwin rather than Lord Curzon as Prime Minister in 1923 confirmed the dominance of the party in the Commons over the leading Conservative families of the peerage, though neither the wealth nor the social background of the Conservative Members of Parliament altered very significantly until the traumatic defeat of the party under Churchill's leadership in 1945. A series of reforms resulted from the investigation of party policy and organization under Lord Woolton and Sir David Maxwell-Fyfe in the late 1940s. Among these were the important provisions for the strict limitation of personal financial contributions from candidates or MPs to constituency funds. This stopped the 'auctioning' of seats to wealthy contenders and allowed a choice of presumably more able candidates to be made, unhampered by financial considerations, and at the same time stimulated constituency associations to raise their finances in other ways. Both in this period and in the years following the 1964 defeat, general improvements were made in communications between constituency associations and party headquarters, and in the representative machinery of the party. Finally, as a result of criticisms arising out of the Macmillan-Home change of leadership in 1963, the party adopted a system of formal election of its Leader, and such an election was the method by which Heath became the present Leader on Home's own resignation.[16]

The *Liberal Party* did not overcome its internal divisions in time to challenge Labour's claim to be the alternative party to the Conservatives, and it lost seats and votes almost uninterruptedly until 1959. A 'revival' followed its improved by-election performances in the 1960s, but the 1964 election (a high-water mark in terms of the $2\frac{1}{2}$ million votes they obtained), by returning Labour, confirmed afresh the third-party status of the Liberals. If Labour had lost its fourth general election in a row, who knows . . . ?

Over the last fifty years, therefore, a two-party system has developed, in which candidates not adopted by one or other of the two parties have little chance of election (other than a handful of mainly Celtic Liberals or an occasional Nationalist), and in which the parties organizationally have become hardly distinguishable one from the other. Labour has taken on some organizational sophistication of the Conservatives, the Conservatives some of the inner-party democracy of Labour. Meanwhile, national policy, party discipline and party finance have become critical organizational factors. The crucial ingredient of leadership will be considered in a later chapter, but now an investigation can be made of the 'what?' of party in Britain – the functions parties perform – and then the 'how?' – the present-day structural organization which enables them to carry out these functions.

[16] See p. 71 below.

3 British political parties:
b. functions and organization

THE FUNCTIONS OF POLITICAL PARTIES: I. THE SEARCH FOR POWER

The most casual listing of answers to the question: 'what do political parties actually do?' would no doubt mention a dozen or more different functions, ranging from the selection of candidates for parliamentary elections to the provision of disciplined support for a government in the House of Commons, from the consideration of party policy on, say, Viet-Nam, to the raising of funds for a general election campaign. Lesser functions might include local government activity, international links with similar parties overseas, social events, nominations for various public offices or committees (e.g. magistracies, consumer councils for public corporations, committees of inquiry), and the training of young people for civic roles through the political youth organizations. But these functions tend to divide into three categories: the inter-related tasks of (i) gaining political power through the electoral system in the central and local government spheres, and (ii) the preparation of policies which the party seeks to realize when in power, along with (iii) a group of miscellaneous subsidiary functions which are to some extent instrumental in furthering the first two, but which might also have a value of their own in the wider context of society as a whole.

That political parties, even in their rudimentary pre-nineteenth-century forms, have always sought power seems evident from their history. This has not always been a search for executive power – in the modern sense of the ability to put a systematic programme into action with the aid of a parliamentary majority. Sometimes it has been power for specific, if much more limited, things – as in the eighteenth and early nineteenth centuries, through the use of influence over King or Queen or royal favourite, or through the exercise of the patronage available to the government. Even in the mid-nineteenth century, minority Conservative governments made large numbers of appointments and created numerous peerages in their brief periods in office, to compensate for fruitless years in opposition, even though they could not pass much controversial legislation through Parliament. The Labour Party, as has been mentioned, was formed in order to give a greater influence to the voice of the 'working-class' in Parliament, but hardly daring to imagine that, within its first sixty years, it would have sufficient power to put through Parliament near-revolutionary programmes of nationalization, provision of social services, and income redistribution on the scale achieved by the Attlee or Wilson administrations.

Indeed, the practice of fighting general elections on the basis of a party programme was only introduced with the increase in important legislative enactments in the second half of the nineteenth century, which created the need for disciplined parties. The possibilities of programmatic legislation encouraged the Radicals (and, in the twentieth century, the Labour and Liberal parties) to put up policy manifestoes at general elections, but some authorities would claim that the Conservatives hardly had an election *programme* (as distinct from a set of pledges of good government) until after the Second World War.

But where power might once have meant other things, today a party asks for a mandate at a general election, not for a single policy, but for a whole range of policies based on a well recognized underlying attitude to society, to government and to the economy. Victory for a party, even if as narrow as the successes of 1950 or 1964, or a victory in terms of seats while coming second in terms of votes, as in 1951 for the Conservatives, is interpreted as a sanction to proceed with a full-scale schedule of legislation for nearly five years – unless by-election defeats erode a narrow majority too far, or electoral tactics suggest a timely renewal of electoral confidence short of the full life of a Parliament. The situation is complicated where more than two parties can hope for governmental power, and then either a minority government stumbles along for a while, restricted severely in its freedom to innovate (Labour in 1924 or 1929–31), or coalitions are formed, with an agreed compromise programme (as with West German governments for most of the period after the resumption of parliamentary democracy in 1949).

Power at the local level may also be important, and the greater proportion of council elections are now fought on party lines. Though central government decisions may limit even such freedom of action by councils as is permitted to them by law (as they have no powers in their own right), and while government economic measures may hinder the ability of councils to proceed with their own policies from time to time, the power which remains with the councils even with such legal and financial restrictions can be worth winning: the controversies over the sale of council houses, or the methods of determining their rent, over comprehensive education or town planning, all illustrate this. Should elected regional councils be introduced by any future reform of local government structure, it seems certain that their control will be another prize for parties to contend for, and this would have an additional effect – so far overlooked even by the parties, it seems – of strengthening the influence of the rather insignificant area or regional party organizations which exist at present.

THE FUNCTIONS OF POLITICAL PARTIES: II. THE MAKING OF POLICY

'Power' as a word is empty of meaning until it is qualified by an answer to the questions: 'Power over whom? to do what?' For parties, the power they seek is power over Parliament by the use of a disciplined majority in order (nowadays) to transform policy demands into statutes. The policies they propose must first be studied and prepared, and the parties are now organized in such a way that they can bring to Parliament policies of a quite detailed nature.

Policies will originate from a variety of sources, in a multiplicity of forms: from the party constitution or manifesto (e.g. nationalization), from the party conference (e.g. the Conservative housing target of 300,000 per year suggested at the 1950 Conference), from response to an initiative taken by the other party (e.g. Gaitskell's highly-qualified Common Market policy in response to the Conservatives' decision to apply for membership of the EEC), from reaction to an external event (e.g.

Wilson's responses to the Rhodesian declaration of independence), from the activities of pressure-groups (e.g. the adoption of a commercial television channel in 1954), or from a stimulus from the departments of the administration (e.g. the breathalyser test), from the back-benches (the abolition of resale price maintenance), from the requirements of alliances (German rearmament), and so forth.

The immediate transmitter of such policies to Parliament is the cabinet (or the shadow cabinet, since the *development* of policy is not confined to periods in office, even if *implementation* usually is, and the decisions to oppose policies of the other party are themselves policies). When necessary, the cabinet can resist considerable amounts of pressure from its back-benchers, its party conference, pressure-groups, or public opinion in its various guises. The cabinet must be responsible for parliamentary strategy, for priorities, for timing, if it is to ensure its continuance in power after the next election. But below the leadership of the parliamentary party, there are quite highly developed channels of communication for informing the leadership of relevant opinion and demands elsewhere. The back-benchers of both parties have regular meetings (the '1922 Committee' for the Conservatives, the Parliamentary Labour Party – the PLP – for Labour). Functional committees exist for the back-benchers of both parties (e.g. on agriculture, defence, foreign affairs). The headquarters of both parties are responsible for relaying information from constituency agents; the representative institutions allow for the expression of opinion from the constituency workers, prospective candidates, affiliated organizations, etc. The Conference itself, though varying from party to party in the degree to which its decisions are binding on the leadership, is an important (if not always very accurate) indicator of party sentiment and current party thinking. The Liberal Assembly for 1964, for example, had as its agenda the draft manifesto for the pending general election, while the notorious defence debates at the Scarborough and Blackpool Conferences of the Labour Party (1960, 1961) demonstrated the importance placed by the Labour leadership on Conference decisions at that time. Even the more autocratic system of Conservative decision-making must take account of Conference, as the sensitivity of the leadership on potentially divisive issues such as Rhodesian independence or comprehensive education has proved.

At local government level, policy decisions are frequently taken at private party gatherings of councillors, and are binding on members to a similar degree as in Parliament, with the same sanctions of refusal of renomination and withdrawal of the whip as operate at Westminster. Policy is derived from the national party programme, local demands, pressures from the local constituency party, and the opinions of the councillors themselves.

THE FUNCTIONS OF POLITICAL PARTIES: III. THE AUXILIARY FUNCTIONS

The search for power, in order to execute policies, would be to the party leaders themselves sufficient reason for the existence of parties, and indeed such an explanation comprehends much of the activity of the parties.

Taking the political system as a whole, however, parties do more than compete for office. Or, rather, such competition produces a spin-off of other socially valuable effects. Indeed, in some countries – examples are China, Russia, Nasser's Egypt, Spain – where only one party exists and political competition takes place, if at all, within the party, many of these other functions of party are illustrated more vividly.

First, the party is a means of political communication and education. Even when a party spokesman is trying to make a case on only one side of an issue, the very act of highlighting the issue conveys its importance to other members of the party, to the opposition, to other interested groups, and to the general public. Any debate which then occurs – in Parliament, on television, in the newspapers, in the council-chamber or civic hall, or on the street corner – will convey information, if of a selective nature. It is true (and particularly so in the one-party states such as the examples just given) that such a process may more properly be called propaganda, but where the parties in a democracy disagree, and where an educated populace and a free press exist, even propaganda will usually be answered in some way. Any number of examples could be given from recent British history, such as the campaign over free trade in 1905–6, when Conservatives favouring selective import duties held meetings up and down the country, with Liberal leaders holding counter-meetings often the very next day in the same town; in more recent times the struggles over nationalization (especially of steel in 1949–50 and 1964–6), nuclear disarmament, and entry into the Common Market are familiar examples. The parties, often after debate within their own organizations, have taken up positions on these issues. Even when these have coincided with the positions of the other party, there has often been opposition from sections of the party, or interest-groups, or the press, which has forced the party to make out a reasoned case, and to publicize it.

Second, the party acts as an organization in which people of various occupations, ages and social backgrounds can take part in political life by actions ranging from the display of an election poster in their front window, or the payment of a nominal party subscription, to canvassing on doorsteps, acting as party officials or even standing as a council or parliamentary candidate. In this way, no section of society needs to feel excluded from political participation or is forced into extra-constitutional action (though protesters, especially of the extreme left or right, have sometimes chosen extra-constitutional methods as being more fruitful, at least in terms of publicity). In this way also, the party hierarchies and Parliament itself, Commons and – since the introduction of Life Peers – Lords, are made more representative. Middle-class grammar school scholars were leading both the main parties involved in the 1966 election; an ex-railwayman was Minister of Labour in the 1964 Labour Government; manual workers who became politicians now sit beside hereditary peers in the Lords; George Brown, once a trade-union official, had as his predecessors in the Foreign Secretaryship such eminent names as Lord Home, Anthony Eden, Lord Halifax, Lord Curzon, Sir Edward Grey and Lord Salisbury. Even in a democratic society, politics still offers one of the more open roads to high position for people lacking wealth, aristocratic birth or university education, though from the small numbers of women MPs or Ministers, it seems that male gender remains a near-essential qualification!

Finally, though this by no means exhausts the list of such subsidiary functions that could be drawn up, a party offers a focus for loyalties and a centre for social life, and these qualities increasingly are coming to be seen as safeguards of democracy as a form of politics. Countries which, having experienced a period of democracy and lost it, have become dictatorships of some kind can generally be found to have possessed weak social groupings below the level of the state and above that of the family or local community. Parties, churches, trade unions, interest groups, are all valuable in the sense of being intermediaries between the individual and the state.

Even before the creation of formal extra-parliamentary organizations in the late nineteenth century, both Conservatives and Liberals had a number of working-men's clubs, especially in the North and Midlands, where political loyalty went hand-in-hand with social and educational activity. Today, many local party headquarters provide, besides an office and sometimes a meeting-hall, a bar, a games room, reading and television rooms, and besides party membership there is often provision for a separate, politically-uncommitted, club membership, a women's section and a youth organization.[1]

A typical week's programme at such a headquarters might include a home match for the darts team in the bar on Monday, a talk on road safety by a police inspector to the youth group on Tuesday, an afternoon coffee meeting for women on Wednesday, followed in the evening by a party committee meeting to discuss the forthcoming borough elections, a bingo session on Thursday for party and club funds, and a busy evening on Friday laying out stalls for Saturday's bring-and-buy sale. The party itself benefits directly from the financial and publicity aspects of such activites, as well as indirectly from the attachment of the participants, if only in the polling-booth at election time. The benefits for the members extend beyond the political into the social sphere. A parallel might be suggested: that of a church. The same variation of activity and degree

[1] One must not underestimate the large numbers of constituency headquarters that do not extend beyond an office, often of the least attractive kind. Many other local parties depend on the use of the Secretary's front room, the occasional hire of a hall, and the storage space of members' attics.

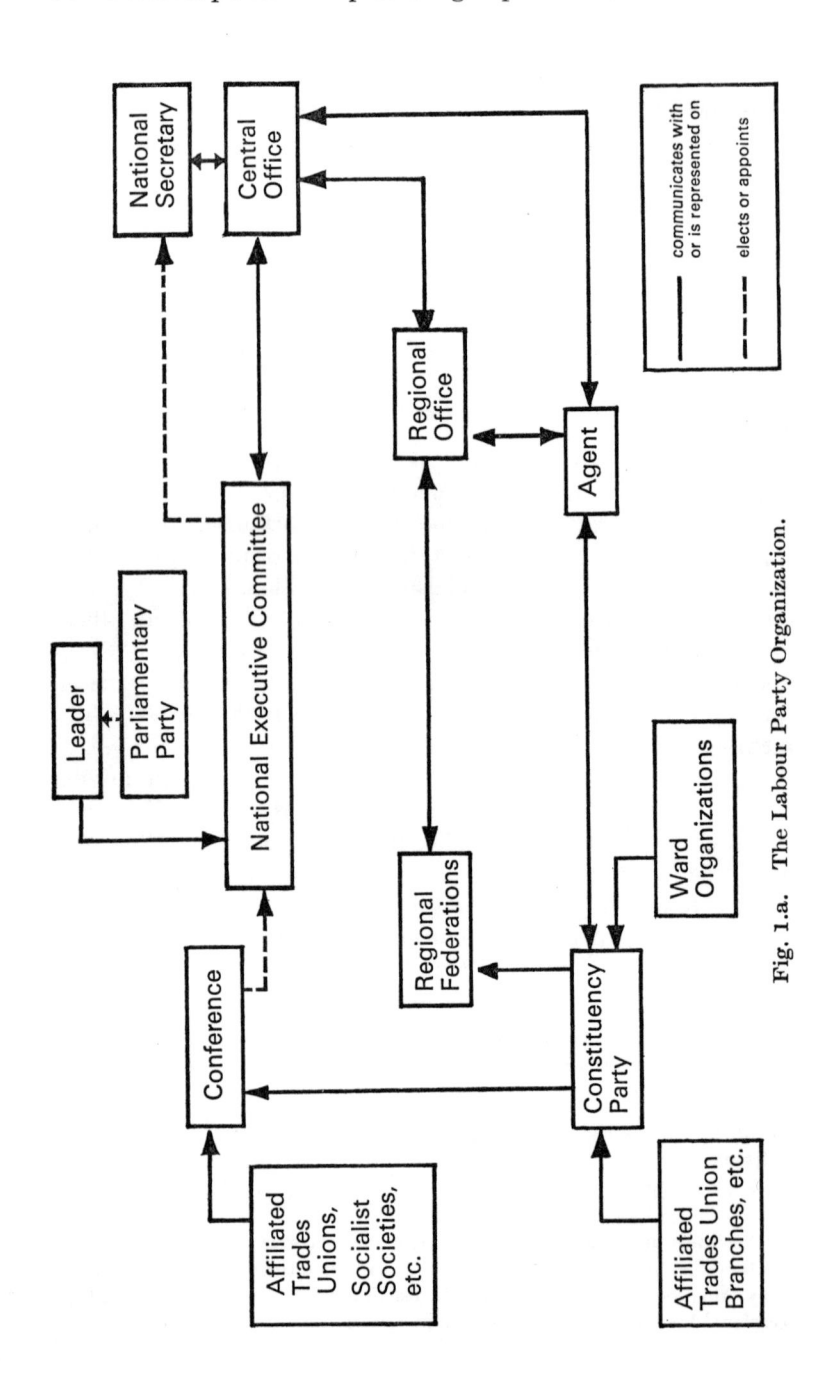

36 *Political parties and pressure groups in Britain*

Fig. 1.a. The Labour Party Organization.

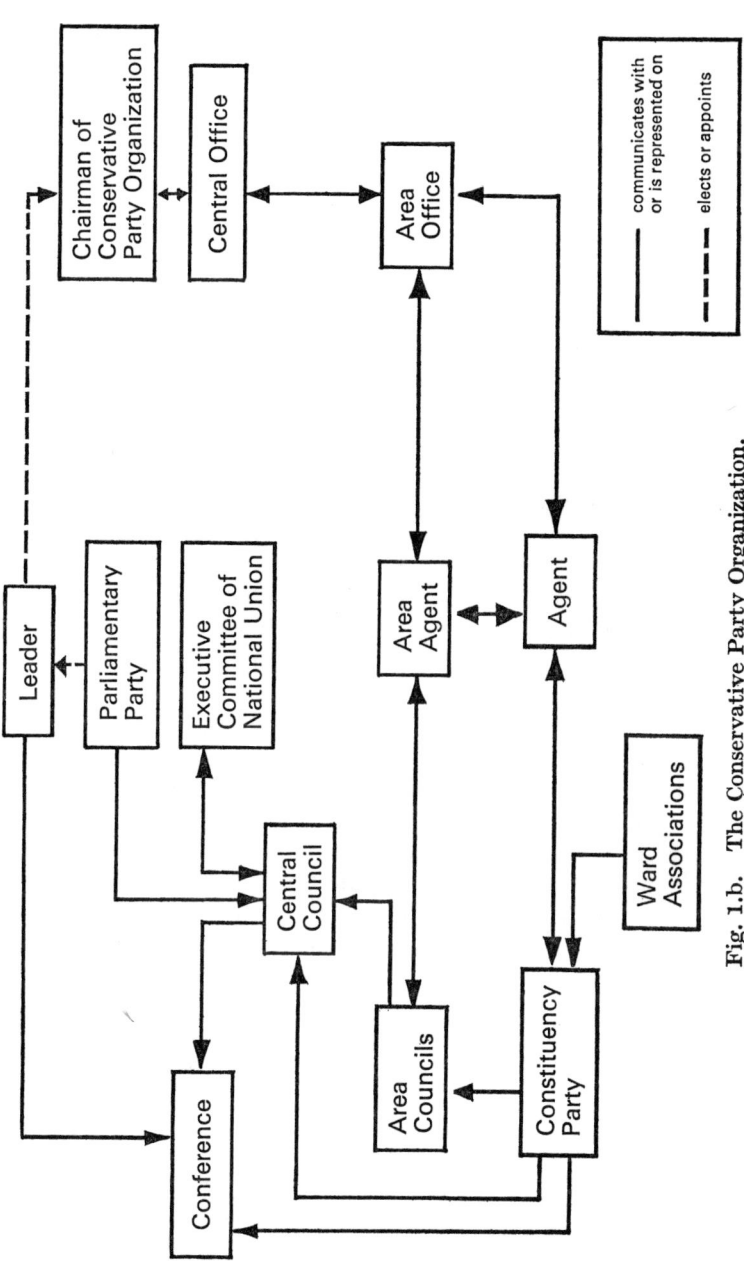

Fig. 1.b. The Conservative Party Organization.

of commitment exists, with the same social effects subsidiary to the main purpose of the institution.

THE ORGANIZATION OF POLITICAL PARTIES

In the Labour, Liberal and Conservative parties – the national mass parties – there are three distinct but closely-related organizations: the parliamentary party, the party bureaucracy, and the representative organizations (see Fig. 1).

The parliamentary organization consists chiefly of the Leader, his front-bench associates (the cabinet or shadow-cabinet), the Chief Whip and his subordinates, the Chairman of the Parliamentary Party in the case of the Labour Party (the chairman of the 1922 Committee[2] in the Conservative Party), and the functional sub-committees which scrutinize and discuss policy in various subject-areas.

The Leader in both major parties[3] is elected by the parliamentary party, and once elected, is extremely powerful if only because he is the Prime Minister or the likely alternative. His duties in connection with Parliament, his national responsibilities, and his policy-making role require him to delegate a considerable proportion of his party duties to his Whips and other colleagues. Nonetheless, at election time the attention of the press, broadcasting and the public is focused on the Leader as the current embodiment of his party's image. There is much debate over the extent to which electoral success is the result of having the 'right type' of Leader – did Macmillan alone win the 1959 election for the Conservatives? or Wilson the 1964 and 1966 elections? It is difficult to deny that at least the Leader is one of the more important factors in election victory or defeat, and the extent of party and press publicity concerning the party Leader is an indication of this. The Leader also has important responsibilities in the bureaucratic and representative organizations, as will be seen below.

[2] So-called because it originated at a famous meeting of Conservative Party MPs and peers which decided to leave the Lloyd George coalition in that year.
[3] The Liberal Party is not significantly different from the other parties in its organization, but in Parliament has less need of complex organization in view of its small representation there.

The front-bench associates of the Leader will derive their importance from two sources: their past experience and seniority within the party – some being Ministers, others ex-Ministers – and, in Opposition, either election to the post of Deputy Leader or to one of the committee posts of the PLP, or appointment by the Conservative or Labour Leader to be a spokesman on, say, defence, or housing, or technology.

The Chief Whip and his assistants are links between the back-bench MPs and the leadership, and play an important part in disciplining recalcitrant Members, and 'keeping a House' (i.e. ensuring that on important matters the party votes its full strength and that, especially on the government side, enough Members attend to allow business to proceed, for instance through an all-night session). They make recommendations to the Leader about suitable candidates for appointment to responsible positions in the party, report on the morale and opinions of the back-benchers, and – an extremely important function – act as the 'usual channels' in Parliament by meeting with their opposite numbers in the other parties to arrange that business in the House goes as smoothly as possible. Nowadays the importance of the post of Chief Whip is recognized by promotion to ministerial positions in many cases: Mr Heath (Leader of the Conservative Party), Mr Short (Postmaster-General) and Lord Bowden (appointed Lord President of the Council in 1964) were all once Chief Whips.

The chairman of the parliamentary party is important because he is, as it were, the 'chief back-bencher'. In the Labour Party he may be an ex-Minister (e.g. Shinwell, or the current chairman,[4] Houghton); in the Conservative Party he is more usually a county Member of long service in Parliament. He is often called upon to convey to the parliamentary leadership the opinions – sometimes the disagreeable opinions – of the parliamentary party. His knowledge of the mood of the party can be of great importance in telling the Leader how far he can go. Before the system of election was introduced in the Conservative Party, he was one of the sources of advice available as to which of the possible candidates should succeed to the

[4] 1969.

office of Leader. This advice was probably given in 1957 (when Macmillan was preferred to Butler) and certainly was in 1963, when Lord Home was chosen to succeed Macmillan.

The functional committees consider pending legislation in their fields, and are at liberty to discuss policy not yet in the form of draft legislation. Membership of one of these committees is useful as experience for a new Member, while the chairmanships are marks of distinction, giving hope of ministerial position in the future. To a limited degree, these committees fill the same function (though without party competition) as do the standing committees of Congress, in the USA, or the German Bundestag, and their importance will increase if the number of parliamentary specialist committees grows, as some reformers wish (at present such parliamentary committees exist for finance, the nationalized industries, agriculture, technology, and statutory instruments). The chief party committees for the 1966–7 Session, for example, were:[5]

> Defence; foreign affairs; finance; Commonwealth affairs; agriculture; Home Office matters; housing and local government; social security; transport; education; power; science and technology; aviation; arts and amenities; legal and judicial (both parties).
> Trade and industry; labour; space; broadcasting (Conservatives only).
> Forestry; trade unions; communications; films; health services; overseas development; public works (Labour only).

In addition, ad hoc and area groups exist as necessary, e.g. the Scottish Unionist Committee or the London Conservative group.

The representative organizations of the parties are based on the constituency party, which may itself be sub-divided into wards and other territorial units. In the Labour Party, in addition to individual membership, local trades-union branches, co-operative and socialist societies, trades councils and similar groups may affiliate to the constituency party. The constituency party works through an executive committee, which

[5] Adapted from A. Roth, *Parliamentary Profiles* (Parliamentary Profile Services, 1966).

usually has decisive power over finance, election campaigns, choice of candidates, etc., subject to approval from the general body of members. Depending on the size of membership, the chances of the party winning the seat, success in local elections, and similar factors, there may be real competition for office within the local party, or it may be more a question of persuading volunteers to assume the tasks of secretary, treasurer, press officer, etc. Depending on the finances available and the work to be done, the local party will employ a full-time or a part-time agent.

The constituency parties are grouped into areas (Conservatives) or regions (Labour). These are co-ordinating and advisory bodies, which also act as an intermediary channel for communication between constituency and party headquarters.

Above this level, the parties have quite distinct forms of representative organization.

The Conservatives have a Central Council, on which sit local representatives, together with adopted candidates, party leaders and officers, and the parliamentary party. In itself, it is a large and unwieldy body, with few important functions, but its 150-strong Executive Committee handles party matters in between meetings of the Central Council, and its sub-committees deal with matters such as the scrutiny of prospective candidates.

The Annual Conference of the Party is generally an uneventful rallying of supporters, with dissension deliberately avoided, though recently party managers have realized that this may be harmful to the party image, and have suggested the encouragement in future of more controversial debates. A recent innovation has been the constant attendance of the Leader throughout the Conference, in place of the dramatic entry at the post-Conference rally on the final day.

Labour has no body corresponding to the National Union's Central Council; its National Executive Committee is a smaller, more powerful body. It is elected for the most part by the sections represented at the Annual Conference, and its composition is:

Leader and Deputy-Leader (ex-officio)	2
Elected by trade-union delegates	12
Elected by constituency delegates	7
Elected by socialist and co-operative delegates	1
Elected by Conference as a whole: women representatives	5
Party Treasurer (elected by Conference)	1
Total	28

This Committee controls party finances, is a disciplinary body (e.g. it can withdraw membership of the party from an individual or an organization), it liaises with the parliamentary party, maintains overall control of party headquarters, endorses candidates and supervises local associations.

The Conference itself conducts a series of often controversial, even bitter, debates, and is theoretically the policy-determining body for the party. In practice, as has been claimed above, the political (as distinct from the formal) powers of the parliamentary leadership, particularly when it is acting as the Government, are now so formidable that Conference has become an influential, rather than a 'sovereign', institution of the party.

The bureaucratic machinery of the two major parties is located in each case in Smith Square, a short stroll from the Houses of Parliament. These headquarters (to quote the Maxwell-Fyfe Report on the Conservative Party, 1948–9) exist 'to guide, inspire and co-ordinate the work of the Party throughout the country, to advise and assist Constituency Associations and Area Councils, and to provide such services as can best be organized centrally'.

Considering the national importance of their responsibilities, the observer must feel disappointed at the lack of professionalism displayed by these organizations, compared to commercial enterprises or to some examples of American and continental party organization. This inefficiency can partly be blamed on lack of finance, partly on the underlying notion that politics is a matter of principle and sacrifice, not professionalism, and partly on the case for efficiency being unappreciated. The two most urgent areas requiring improvement are communications (including advertising) and personnel. The attempts to 'democratize' the Conservative Party in 1945–50, and the improvements of party communications following the 1963 Selwyn Lloyd Report only made an anachronistic pattern into something more up-to-date. The hiring of a professional advertising agency (Colman, Prentis and Varley) in 1957 was a further step forward, and one which Labour was forced to emulate, at least in part, after the 1959 election. But in all three party organizations misunderstandings, confusion and duplication of effort still exist. The problem of employing and retaining skilled personnel is partly financial, in that salaries are often well below comparable payments obtainable in other posts, and partly a lack of status: consider the number of valued party officials who have sought parliamentary careers: Peter Shore (now in the Cabinet), David Ennals, Iain Macleod, John Biffen, and the candidate who failed to prevent Orpington falling to the Liberals, Peter Goldman.

The Conservative organization is headed by a Chairman (who may be an MP, a peer, or even from outside Parliament) who is appointed by the Leader. As well as efficiency, personal compatibility with the Leader must play some part in his appointment: the substitution of Anthony Barber for Edward du Cann (1967) may be an illustration of this. The Central Office itself is divided into an Organizational Department (responsible for constituency, financial, electoral and organizational matters) and departments dealing with publicity, speakers, industrial matters, local government, and the Young Conservative organization. Because of his wide and important responsibilities, the Chairman must necessarily possess considerable influence in party matters, and will be an important source of information for the Leader concerning morale and opinion in the party nationally. The area offices are branch offices of Headquarters, and act as an intermediary level of organization.

The key professional politician in the party is undoubtedly the local Agent. His importance is often unrecognized except by his constituency MP or candidate, and the more perceptive of the local elected officers of the party. The Conservatives have full-time Agents in five-sixths of the constituencies, and a recently-revised salary scale now extends from £900 for a young Agent up to something over £2,000 per year, plus a car, expenses and a pension scheme. The party has also appointed some Cadet Agents (school-leavers with 'O' level GCE) and has a thorough examination and training system. In some constituencies, the Agent may be the person with most influence in selection procedures for candidates[6] and is generally very knowledgeable politically, though there is a tendency for him to be so overburdened with everyday financial and organizational matters that he cannot give as much attention as he would wish to political practice.

Labour Headquarters in Transport House is under the control of the National Executive Committee (see above), who appoint a Secretary to run the day-to-day affairs of the party outside Parliament. The departments are remarkably similar to those of Conservative Central Office: a Secretary's Department, and sections dealing with research, organization, women, finance, publicity, and international matters. Regional staff are also appointed by the National Executive Committee.

Labour has far fewer full-time Agents in the constituencies than the Conservative Party – probably no more than 250 (the Liberals have probably about fifty). Their salaries are lower, and in many cases they hold elected positions in local government also, unlike their Conservative counterparts.

Academic studies and practical experience alike demonstrate the importance in party organization and operation of two factors: historical tradition and ideology. Institutional arrangements become associated with political belief to a remarkable extent – the furore over the alteration of the method of choosing the Conservative Leader is an example. Other traditions continue because they *are* traditional, irrespective of their efficiency in any sense at all. Some, such as the near-automatic renomination of sitting Members, may have valuable consequences, in this case in terms of loyalty, local sympathies, and the attraction of a 'safe seat' as an incentive to a young candidate to fight hopeless seats first; others, such as the eve-of-poll meeting, the election address, the party conference, local selection of candidates and doorstep canvassing have not been examined functionally by the parties themselves. Do these things divert scarce resources

[6] A. Ranney, *Pathways to Parliament* (Macmillan, 1965), pp. 72–73.

(and they are scarce!) from more effective methods of publicity, communication, encouragement of the faithful or the stimulation of voters? Would not perhaps an investment of 1 per cent or 5 per cent of the election budget of headquarters be better used in the long term in a survey, not of voters' opinions, since these may be fickle or even irrelevant when considering the effectiveness of electoral tactics, but of operating efficiency, of costly institutions and practices, and the consideration of alternatives? Does it not rest with the parties – so critical of inefficiency in governmental, commercial or trade union organizations – to put their own practices in order?

The one incentive to such re-examination seems to be electoral defeat. The Conservatives, shocked by Churchill's failure to beat the Socialists in 1945 as he had beaten the Axis Powers, conducted a thorough investigation and reorganization in 1946–50 concerning party procedure, policy and communication. David Maxwell-Fyfe, who was responsible for suggesting many of these changes in his Report to the party in 1948–9, wrote of them thus:

The Report had several important minor effects, but its main results were the establishment of a system of trained, paid, and experienced agents throughout the country, the absolute removal of financial burdens upon candidates, the careful definition of the roles of the various party organizations to ensure that there was no serious overlapping of effort or mutual jealousies – which had caused considerable difficulties in the past – and the unequivocal endorsement of the independence of the constituency organization, particularly in the selection of candidates.[7]

A similar, if less revolutionary examination was initiated after the 1966 election result.

Labour also found election defeat traumatic. Gaitskell's battles with the left-wing over Clause IV (which he wished to revise) – the clause imposing apparently unlimited nationalization on all Labour's programmes, and subscription to which remains a requirement of party membership – and over nuclear disarmament, can be attributed in large measure to the 1959 election result, the third successive, and largest postwar, victory for the Conservatives. Harold Wilson conducted a

[7] Lord Kilmuir, *Political Adventure* (Weidenfeld & Nicolson, 1964), p. 158.

post-1959 inquiry into the organization of the party – which he termed a penny-farthing machine. The survey conducted by Mark Abrams after the 1959 defeat (*Must Labour Lose?*)[8] also stimulated a review of the presentation of the party image and party policy.

THE PARTY PROGRAMME

What is it all for? The complicated machinery of the parties, the multiple offices, organizations, centres of decision, and sources of policy, the hundreds of thousands of pounds and the millions of voters at each election – what is the end product?

The answer is: a programme and a government, chosen by the electorate from the alternatives presented to them by the parties. To some, this would be a fairly satisfactory definition of the word 'democracy', but that is a wider question to be treated elsewhere in this book.

The programmes may be ambiguous, generalized, and over-loaded with pledges to each and every interest; the promises may remain unfulfilled – through lack of parliamentary time, insufficient resources, a lack of party enthusiasm, public opposition, or the exigencies of the day; new, unforeseen policies may become necessary; but basically the differences between what the parties stand for, between what they are likely to do when in office, are contained in their election manifestoes. An examination of the manifestoes of the three major parties at the 1966 election is thus of some interest.[9]

The Liberals' booklet – *For All The People* – criticized the other parties as tied to the interests of capital and the unions, whereas the Liberals draw support from 'all groups and classes'. A chronicle of the benefits of Liberal pressure in the 1964–6 Parliament followed, including the postponement of steel nationalization, increases in pensions, and attention for the regions and the ratepayers. The next section, entitled 'How to create the wealth', proposed reductions in defence commitments overseas, entry into the Common Market, simplification of the tax system, cuts in direct taxation, lower

[8] Penguin, 1960.
[9] Other aspects of these manifestoes are considered below, Chapter 6, 'Groups and Policy'.

prices, a positive incomes policy to encourage job mobility, co-partnership and increased status for employees, expansion of farming, a plan for the regions, radical changes in transport policy, and modernization of the civil service machine and Parliament, including electoral reform, since 'a system which allowed over three million voters only nine Members of Parliament . . . is clearly in need of a radical overhaul'.

Then follow suggestions on 'How to improve our way of life'. These include the use of industrialized building techniques, and other policies to keep down rates, to reduce the housing shortage, improvements in social security and the health service (financed by a regionally variable social security tax), priority for education and support for international organizations. In conclusion, the party summed up its policy in these terms:

> We want to see positive action to create a close partnership between all sections of the Community – state and private enterprise, employer and employee, business and union – only we can bring about this partnership.

Action not words was the title of the 'new Conservative programme'. Faced with the need to present a new series of policies to an electorate which, only eighteen months previously, had shown its disillusionment with thirteen years of Conservative government, yet unable and unwilling to disavow the achievements of those governments, Mr Heath in a foreword emphasized economic strength as his priority, mentioning also the removal of 'the growing constraint of Socialism', selective development of the social services, and entry into the Common Market. The programme itself was specific about priorities, starting with this list:

> This is what we are going to do:
> Get the economy straight, check rising prices, and restore expansion
> Reform the trade unions
> Remodel the Welfare State
> Get the nation properly housed
> Restore respect for Britain and lead her into Europe

Complaints about 'The Labour Record' were followed by

'The Conservative Way Ahead', in which the earlier list of priorities is expanded, laying emphasis on tax incentives for individuals, new policies for competition, reform for management and unions, prosperity for the regions and expansion of exports, the concentration of state benefits 'on those most in need', a housing target of half a million homes a year, and improvements in education, transport, prevention of crime, the countryside, and the machinery of government.

The remaining pages set out these aims in a yet more specific fashion, as a 'Blueprint for a Parliament'. Under the heading 'to improve industrial relations', for instance, come proposals like these:

> Pass a new Industrial Relations Act and establish a new Code of Good Industrial Relations Practice.
> Ensure that agreements between unions and employers are kept by making them legally enforceable.
> Set up a new Industrial Court to deal with industrial disputes and claims for damages against unjust dismissal.

Labour's manifesto was called *Time for Decision*. A preface appealed for a renewed and strengthened mandate for the 'radical reconstruction of our national life' which was started in 1964. The opening section blamed the Conservatives for the financial crisis which had arisen in 1964 and praised the achievements of Labour's 500 days in office. Then came a section on 'A Strong Economy', dealing with the balance of payments, productivity, industrial and agricultural policy. A plan for 'Building a New Britain' gave first priority to houses (like the Conservatives, a target of 500,000 was proposed), then emphasized urban renewal, the National Transport Plan, and schemes for the countryside. Social services naturally received considerable emphasis, and detailed proposals were given for full employment policies, reconstructing the social services and education, as well as policies for leasehold enfranchisement, rents, council tenants, and a mortgage subsidy scheme. Taxation and rate reforms were also mentioned.

Like the other parties, policies were suggested for reorganizing Whitehall, modernizing Parliament, and strengthening law enforcement, while the final section dealt with defence, Commonwealth and international affairs. A postscript reiterated the need for a working majority in Parliament to further 'our plan for a better Britain'.

The dilemma faced by all three parties may be summarized thus: (i) for the Liberals: how to give credibility to policies that would be neither 'Conservative' nor 'Socialist' in tone, yet which stood little chance of being effected by a Liberal Government in the foreseeable future; (ii) for the Conservatives: how to present a novel programme, yet avoid the charge of 'why didn't you do this when in office?'; (iii) for Labour: how to differentiate its policies from those of Liberals or moderate Conservatives, and yet avoid alarming the 'middle-of-the-road' voter with too much 'Socialism'; (iv) for all parties: how to capture the essential middle ground of the political battlefield, yet retain the enthusiasm and the assistance of the party activists, who often regarded themselves as the guardians of 'Socialism', 'radical Liberalism' or 'true Conservatism' – in other words tended to be more extreme than were the voters which the party intended to attract.

The manifestoes revealed these dilemmas in many ways. All three contain much in the way of common policy – more housing, regionalism, entry into Europe, international cooperation, priority for education, reorganization of the social services. The Liberals appealed for a 'stronger influence' on the party in power, in the name of the people who did not belong to the 'vested interests' of unions or capitalism. The Conservatives, with only a brief passage of criticism of the Labour Government, focused on action and a set of priorities, avoiding many matters which might be contentious within the party. Labour tried to justify its own policies by criticizing the Conservative record – phrases such as the 'Tory swindle' on pensions, the 'evil effects of the 1962 Tory Transport Act', recur throughout the manifesto.

Despite these problems, it must be remembered that Labour's majority in 1966 depended on a net switch of about three voters in every 100 who voted Conservative in 1964, and that for the bulk of the voters it was not the manifesto, not the candidate, not the election campaign that influenced their choice, but a general image that they possessed of the Tory, Liberal and Labour parties. modified by their assessment of the records of recent Conservative and Labour governments.

4 British political parties: c. leaders and followers

The study of leaders and the ways in which they exercise power is at the very heart of politics. Whether one ranges through history – Alexander the Great, Julius Caesar, Napoleon, Bismarck, Hitler, Stalin, Churchill – or among the leaders of the hundred or more states that make up the post-war international system – Kennedy, Castro, de Gaulle, Nkrumah, Mao Tse-Tung – the lives and deeds of such men, whether for good or evil, are the core of political history, while the arts, as well as political science, have been concerned with the fascination of political leadership. Consider the many plays of Shakespeare that have a political figure as the centre of action, the many novels that have been written about the exploits of the Caesars or Napoleon, the painters and sculptors who have, voluntarily or by commission, represented the likenesses of leaders, the musicians and poets who have taken inspiration from subjects connected with political leadership.

Nor is it only the successful leader who has provided an interesting subject for historians and biographers. Those who struggled to achieve leadership, yet, for various reasons, failed to attain it, are almost equally inviting as central figures. In recent British history, who can peruse the biographies of, say, Dilke, Lord Curzon, or Rab Butler without wondering what kind of Premiers they would have been, had it not been for scandal, or personality differences, or the rapid rise to high office of a rival? Is not part of the tragedy of such men as Trotsky, Adlai Stevenson, Nye Bevan or Robert Kennedy the fact that circumstances denied them the chance of using their undoubted talents in the highest offices of political leadership of their countries?

Organizations need leaders. States, being generally the most complex of human organizations, rely heavily on the exercise of leadership. Yet, though the histories of individual leaders have been written over and over again, their more general qualities have received relatively little attention, while important questions such as the relationship between leaders and followers, the methods by which political leaders are recruited, trained and prepared for their eminent responsibilities, how different styles of leadership affect the working of institutions such as political parties, and how leaders are changed one for another, have also been neglected. These questions have concerned thinkers about political problems from Plato onwards, but each society has, to some extent, to ask them of itself with every new generation, because the answers will change with changes within society itself.

It is obvious that, in a representative democracy such as Britain, where theoretically at least, ultimate power lies with the citizen-electors, and actual power is shared among many institutions – the Cabinet, Parliament, the civil service, local government, as well as parties and pressure-groups – these questions about leadership are more important than they would be in, for example, a feudal monarchy or a dictatorship. There is a built-in distrust of leadership in a democracy, and, some may say, even a discouragement of it. Social and economic egalitarianism must have an effect of encouraging political egalitarianism also. 'I'm as good as he is, any day' is not an uncommon remark in referring to the Prime Minister, his colleagues in the Cabinet, or their opponents in the other parties. It is not easy to encourage the individual civic responsibilities of the citizen, and simultaneously to provide him with the notion of the necessity of leadership. This is one of the perpetual political problems of our society. On the other hand, surveys have demonstrated the survival of widespread attitudes of 'deference' among the electorate, who place qualities of 'strong leadership' high on their list of expectations in a leader.[1]

A word of definition, then, before looking more closely at the ways in which problems of leadership are managed in Britain. The term 'leaders' as used in this chapter will refer primarily to the men in politics who are Leaders of their parties as Prime Minister, Leader of the Opposition, or of the Liberals in Parliament, and to their principal colleagues, i.e. what is often called the 'front-bench'. When it is necessary to refer to

[1] See, e.g. M. Abrams, *et alia*, *Must Labour Lose?* (Penguin, 1960).

others, for example outside Parliament, who may be regarded as possessing special influence within the parties, this will be specified.

THE QUALITIES OF LEADERSHIP

Opinions differ as to what the qualities of a British political leader should be. This is not surprising, since leaders in the past have possessed a variety of different qualities, lacking some altogether, yet strong in others. How different was Attlee from Churchill, for example, in his methods and his personality! Similar sharp contrasts can be found earlier in our history: Gladstone, emphasizing the moral force of leadership, and Disraeli, emphasizing its glamour; Asquith, the careful lawyer, possessed of the power to persuade men through argument, and Lloyd George, the flamboyant politician, with the power to persuade men through passion; nearer to the present, the contrasts between the public-school and Oxford-educated Gaitskell and the self-educated product of the Welsh mining valleys, Bevan, were equally marked.

Certain obvious prerequisites would suggest the possession of some minimum abilities. Leaders of parties nowadays will certainly have shown the ability to be selected as candidates and to fight several elections successfully, in order to possess the parliamentary experience necessary to their being chosen as Leader. Consider the record of post-war Leaders:

Leader	*Party*	*First entered Parliament*	*Selected as Leader*
Thorpe	Lib.	1959	1967
Heath	Con.	1950	1965
Home	Con.	1931	1963
Wilson	Lab.	1945	1963
Macmillan	Con.	1924	1957
Grimond	Lib.	1950	1956
Eden	Con.	1923	1955
Gaitskell	Lab.	1945	1955
Clement Davies	Lib.	1929	1945
Churchill	Con.	1900	1940
Attlee	Lab.	1922	1935

Added to their electoral abilities will be qualities of wisdom, displayed in debate in Parliament, in speeches outside it, in committees, at party conferences, and perhaps in published writings. Such 'policy skills' as the craft of negotiation, the techniques of persuasion, and the ability to take a firm decision, will, when added to some expertise in certain areas of public policy – defence, social services, foreign affairs, the economy, parliamentary reform, – constitute a strong claim to ministerial rank (or equivalent status in the opposition parties).

But something extra is required before the journalists include a particular politician in their periodic speculations on 'The Next Prime Minister'. It is a quality that is elusive, difficult to describe, though words such as 'heft', 'credibility', or 'weight' (or the Latin equivalent *gravitas*) are sometimes used. To call it the 'quality of leadership' is tautology; nevertheless it is the ability to project oneself as a believeable leader that matters. There are many examples of prominent politicians who failed to impress their colleagues in this way. They may have possessed everything else: electoral popularity, administrative ability, policy expertise, wit, intellect, connections, even personal charm, yet for one reason or another the idea of their leading the party was impossible to accept. Some of the names suggested in connection with Macmillan's retirement could be cited as examples. In its more extreme form, this quality has been called 'charisma', and it is precisely because leaders must project their leadership, especially in a representative system, that it is so important an attribute.

Not all party Leaders had opportunity to display talents of leadership in advance of their elevation, though. Neither Attlee nor Home could be regarded as having done so, despite their other qualities. Certainly both developed leadership characteristics that were unsuspected before. Like the White House in America, the leadership of a British political party somehow forces occupants to 'grow into' the demands of the office.

Leadership is one thing; successful leadership is something more. In a democracy, at least, leaders must possess integrity, the courage to take responsibility for unpopular decisions (and the greater courage to alter such decisions once they are proved unsuited to the circumstances), a sense of strategy, so that every issue is not made a matter of party conflict, and, most of all, the talent of communication – the art of getting hold of important information in time, and of being able to explain convincingly why decisions have been taken.

WHY DO MEN WANT TO BE LEADERS?

Despite the demands such qualifications impose on aspirants to leadership, there is never a lack of candidates for the highest party positions. A pessimistic observer might despair of discovering a paragon of sufficient merit to match the near-Platonic standards which have just been catalogued, yet, despite the rarity of 'philosopher-kings' in real life, so far the British democracy has found its leaders, and has discovered in them more than a modicum of leadership talents. But the intriguing question of *why* men are prepared to undertake the most demanding political positions in the country is not easily answered.

A taste for the exercise of power is one reason; as the Presidency was for John Kennedy, the Premiership can be very much an opportunity to carry out programmes with powers denied to occupants of lesser offices. This self-confidence is very necessary, and its lack would soon show through, as happened to Neville Chamberlain in the first crises of the war in 1940. A sense of civic obligation is another reason. Men offer themselves for leadership in the party battle for the same reason that other men accept judgeships, assignments to committees of inquiry, seats on the magisterial bench, or nomination for council elections – because, whether the prestige or the material rewards be great or small, a sense of duty demands it.

Political conviction can also be important. Men who have given a lifetime of effort to a cause in which they believe must welcome the opportunity to direct that cause personally, whether they believe that they are pressing forward to a Socialist Britain, bringing Conservatism up-to-date, or revivifying Liberalism. Secondary reasons may be found in abundance: family tradition (e.g. the Cecils, the Stanleys and the Churchills), dislike of a rival who might otherwise attain leadership by default, the lack of an alternative Leader who can find general acceptance in the Party (an important element, presumably, in Home's decision to accept the Conservative leadership in 1963), pressure from ambitious supporters (who were not lacking when Lloyd George replaced Asquith, for instance, in 1916), and so on. But, whatever the reasons might be, they must be balanced by consideration of the costs of leadership.

Such costs begin to accumulate long before the moment of decision arrives. They include the costs of entering, and persisting in, politics as a career. It is only recently that the salary of an MP came to be increased to the level of some of the other professions. Even at a salary of £3,250, an ambitious and talented MP will probably be earning several hundred pounds less than he could in commerce or in a free profession such as law or accountancy, or perhaps even in the capacity of a civil servant. True, many Members add to their parliamentary salaries through part-time practice of a profession, or through journalism, but the former may well detract from the full-time attention to political matters that is expected of an aspirant to high political office (and is not available to Ministers, who have only a moderately increased salary), while the other is only well-paid when the author has generally spent some years in Parliament, and gained a reputation for unorthodoxy that is greater, or better-publicized, than that expected of a party leader. Among such able writers are Michael Foot, Desmond Donnelly and Iain MacLeod – none of them at present seriously considered as credible alternatives to their leaders. The fringe benefits of more secure employment are missing also. Ex-premiers are pensioned, and ex-Members of Parliament may, under certain circumstances, draw a pension on retirement after at least ten years' service, but this is still small (£600 p.a. after ten years, £900 p.a. after fifteen years' service, and an extra £24 p.a. for each additional year). Only on leaving politics can political experience command its premium, for instance in commerce or the professions.

Physical and social costs are less easy to estimate, but there is every reason to suppose that the health and the family life of the politician are affected by his vocation. George Brown, in an article on his resignation from Harold Wilson's Cabinet, emphasized how much he looked forward to having the chance to take up interests outside politics, and have a social life again.[2] Long hours of work, all-night sittings, the travel and hurried meals involved in visits to his constituency, the strains of publicity, the unhelpful conditions in which he performs his tasks at Westminster – these affect every Member who takes his work seriously. For the party Leader, and especially for the Prime Minister, they multiply in force. The hours lengthen – he is an MP, chief Minister, and party Leader as well, yet his day has only as many hours as before. He nurses his constituency – which is not necessarily safer because of his exalted position (consider the 1966 majorities of Mr Heath at Bexley, or Mr Thorpe at North Devon, and the handful of Ministers and ex-Ministers who lose their seats at each general election). He is daily in the public eye, even on holiday. He must travel extensively throughout Britain, and is frequently required to travel abroad – Washington, the European capitals, Moscow, the Commonwealth – perhaps at very short notice. In 1969, only Eden, Macmillan and Home are still living of British ex-Premiers, and the first two of these retired on grounds of ill-health requiring important surgical treatment. Only Jo Grimond survives of ex-party Leaders who never reached the Premiership. Of course, men tend to come into the leadership at a mature age, but this role of leadership implies increasing physical strain at an age when men in other professions are thinking of abandoning burdens of office, rather than increasing them.

And the loneliness? The isolation? The need for meticulous treatment of friends, to avoid suspicion of favouritism? The extreme unpleasantness of 'being a butcher' and telling colleagues of long standing and of valuable past service that for various reasons their resignations are required? Clement Attlee said this about such a problem:

> It's awkward to have to sack a man and tell him he doesn't make the grade. But I always think it's best to tell him so frankly, not rush around looking for some sort of cushion for him, like telling him it isn't his fault but you happen to need a man with some other sort of experience and you'll try to fit him into some other job later. I don't think that's playing straight with a fellow. If he doesn't

[2] See his article in the *Sunday Times*, 17 March 1968.

measure up to the job, you should tell him. It's unpleasant, but it's a job a Prime Minister must do for himself.[3]

Such costs as these are perhaps impossible to measure, but the glib reply of the boy when asked what he wishes to be when he grows up: 'Prime Minister!', may turn into regret from a fatigued occupant of 10 Downing Street that the more orthodox career of an engine-driver was not chosen instead. At least the engine-driver would not have to quell rebellions from the passengers about the route to be taken, nor suspect his guard of one day attempting to take over the controls!

The ultimate cost is the need to accept retirement or defeat, perhaps when still confidently capable of exercising leadership. Unlike the retired general, the director of ICI, or the professor who can become 'emeritus', there is rarely a satisfactory substitute career available for the ex-Prime Minister or the ex-Leader. He must observe the blunders – or, worse, the successes – of his replacement. He must be strict in not offering advice, unless it is specifically requested as coming from an 'elder statesman'. Congenial occupations are available, of course – the mastership of an Oxbridge College, control of the family firm left some years before, the conceit of memoir-production. But any potential Leader must be aware, in a democracy, that his primary career may be over long before he is ready to relinquish it.

One strange aspect of acquiring a position of political leadership is the extreme shift in popular estimation of status that results. While the 'politician' is likely to be regarded as a self-seeking, conceited, ill-informed careerist, not to be compared with respectable professional classes such as architects, accountants, barristers, civil servants or physicians, the Prime Minister, his chief colleagues and chief opponents become 'statesmen', men of esteem and integrity, fit to represent the nation. Possibly the fact that the Queen appoints ministers has much to do with it, along with frequent appearances on television or in the press, often in a national rather than a partisan role, so that they become at once more familiar, yet more exalted, in the opinion of the man in the street. The numerous recent satirical publications, television and theatrical

[3] F. Williams, *A Prime Minister Remembers* (Heinemann, 1961), p. 85.

productions have had an impact on politics exceeding their intrinsic merits, because they have gone counter to this trend, and have treated leaders as suitable targets for humour and for criticism. In some circumstances, such as the last years of the Weimar Republic in Germany, this has been a symptom of public alienation from the regime; in Britain it can be regarded (at the present, at least) as another indication of the rooted strength of representative democracy, despite changes in the popularity of particular leaders or governments.

WHO ARE THE LEADERS?

Some definitions of democracy would include the qualification that leaders should be chosen by the people in free elections, and should be representative of them. If the people's choice is limited to selection from a small group, qualified by class, wealth, education or similar characteristics, this limits democracy itself in some measure. Others would claim that mere 'mirror representation' of the population is irrelevant to the task of government – indeed, can be positively harmful in that it allows the mediocre to replace the well-qualified – and has nothing whatsoever to do with the problem of representing the wishes of the electorate. For the first group, the language of their criticism contains words like 'establishment', 'oligarchy' and 'meritocracy', while the second group talks of 'elites', the 'profession of politics' and 'democratic leadership'.

The problem of representation has exercised the minds of many thinkers over the centuries. The well-known speech of Burke, to his Bristol electorate, when he proclaimed that he would gladly be their representative, but never merely their delegate, is an example of the arguments of those who claim that representation should not remove the dignity of a leader by confining him to the role of mouthpiece for his followers.

But authoritative instructions, mandates issued, which the member is bound blindly and implicitly to obey, to vote and to argue for, though contrary to the clearest conviction of his judgment and conscience – these are things, utterly unknown to the laws of this land, and which arise from a fundamental mistake of the whole order and tenor of our Constitution.[4]

[4] Speech to the Electors of Bristol, 1774.

Others have seen in this claim a danger that politicians elected to Parliament would employ their 'conscience' as an excuse to thwart the wishes of the people. The growth of political parties has added a new dimension to the debate, for not only is there now the question of how representative are party leaders (and hence the government or alternative governments), but also the problem of the process of representation within the procedures and institutions of party itself (and this will be considered later in this chapter).

So the issues are these: assuming that Britain should be governed as a representative democracy, *what* should be represented? By *whom*? And *how* should representatives be chosen?

The first question cannot be answered simply by saying: 'The people', for 'the people' are so varied in themselves. They are dispersed geographically, and it is often overlooked that the one principle of representation sanctioned by constitutional law (subject to very minor qualifications) is geographical location. We elect an MP for a constituency that is defined in terms of physical area. It may gain population, or lose it; it may change from agricultural to residential, or residential to industrial in use; it may grow more prosperous, or become a depressed area; it may experience an influx of working-class Londoners over-spilled into a middle-class market town, or the inflow of immigrants from the Commonwealth, or the establishment of a new University, or the closure of the local railway-line – no matter how it changes, the principle of local representation (subject to periodic revision by the Boundary Commissioners and Parliament) is the only one recognized by law. Party, interest, economic characteristics, social change – none of these are taken into account by the various Acts governing the Representation of the People. The elimination of university representation in 1948 completed this process.

A complication – an anomalous complication, assert the reformers – is the House of Lords, which represents in law only the Lords themselves, not 'the people'. Yet this does not really affect the problem of what the leadership of the parties represents, for few members of recent Cabinets (other than Lord Chancellors) have been Peers.

The law says that an MP represents a constituency, and, to

be fair, in practice the MP generally seeks to represent the interests of his constituency when these are involved either as a local matter (such as the rebellion of some Conservatives from London or suburban constituencies over the London Government Bill, or the opposition of local MPs to the Stansted airport proposals), or in personal cases. But in terms of political realities, it is generally accepted that MPs are elected as supporters of political parties, and that elections are decided in national terms by which of the party leaders can, after the results are in, claim a majority of the elected MPs as his supporters. In turn, the parties represent primarily economic orientations to the problems which are expected to be solved by political means, though there are still some perceptible social differences between them over e.g. penal reform, race relations, internationalism, and education policy. In general, though, Labour stands for a more equitable distribution of national wealth, the generous provision of social services by state agencies, control of key industries and commercial institutions by public, rather than private, managerial boards, and centralized economic direction of quite a high order, while the Conservatives emphasize freedom of economic institutions with a minimum of state regulation, the increase of national wealth so that individuals can more easily make their own provisions for social services, removal of as much state economic control as possible, and the distribution of national wealth (subject to provision for basic minimum needs) by economic forces rather than state planning. Liberals regard state and private monopolies as equally dangerous, and seek to democratize and decentralize decision-making in both the economic and political spheres, while ensuring that a decent standard of living is available to all – by co-operation if possible, by state provision if not.

As well as their party affiliation, some Members represent interests (e.g. religious denominations) or pressure-groups (e.g. the Mineworkers' Union, the British Legion), but this representation is subsidiary to party claims, and is fortuitous to the extent that such representation is dependent upon selection and election procedures over which the interests have only a small degree of influence, if any at all. Some seats are regarded as miners' or railwaymen's seats, because of the preponderant strength of their union in the constituency Labour party, and among the electorate. But other interests, other groups, even when possessed of considerable national resources and membership, are rarely, in any one constituency, sufficiently concentrated to affect the election result, and are even less likely to be in a position to influence the party choice of a particular candidate.

Proposals have been made from time to time to include a measure of interest or 'functional' representation within the British political system. Those who argue in favour claim that a person's occupation, religion, leisure interests, and organizational affiliations are at least as important to him (in national terms) as his location or his social class. A person may well move up and down the country as he advances in his chosen profession or vocation, yet his influence on national decisions will be based on his variable location of residence rather than his occupational interests as lawyer, docker, teacher, local government administrator, salesman or motorway engineer. To remedy this, such proposals focus on the direct representation of interests in Parliament, and some of these schemes of reform suggest changing the House of Lords into a 'Council of Interests' in some form. Even supposing such a scheme were acceptable in principle (and one cannot imagine the parties agreeing to such a reduction in their own status) major problems remain, such as the basis of representation – how many trade unionists? From which unions? How many Church of England clergy? How many Catholic clergy? How many doctors? Should they be general practitioners, surgeons, or consultants? Who would choose, and how? What powers would such a chamber possess? and so on.

It may be assumed that the parties themselves will be forced, by their need to secure votes, to represent all the important aspects of national life, but one may still question whether there should be a closer correspondence between the social characteristics of the population, and those of the MPs and party leaders. There are, for example, far fewer women in the Commons, the Cabinet or the Opposition front-bench than in the electorate as a whole. The average age of party leaders – and MPs – seems to be high, giving rise to questions of the representation of the generations.

	Population[5]	MPs[6]	Leaders[7]
	(expressed as percentages)		
Men	47	96	89
Women	53	4	11
21–39 years old	36	22	6
40–59 years old	38	61	80
60+ years old	26	17	14

Charges of 'unrepresentative leadership' usually concentrate on two other factors – occupation and social class. These complaints are to some degree more valid, in that a government may be said to require the inclusion of a certain range of experience in order to be able to appreciate the demands of the population and the effects of particular policies on the electorate. Yet the leadership of all three parties, Labour, Conservative and Liberal, tends to be overwhelmingly upper- or middle-class, well-educated, and with experience in only a very limited range of occupations – chiefly the law, business direction or management, education, party or trade union administration, and the armed forces. Consider the background of a sample list of thirty leading politicians in 1968:

Labour. Bowden – commerce; Brown – trade-union organizer; Castle – journalist; Crosland – academic economist; Healey – journalist, broadcaster; Jenkins – economic consultant; Shore – party official; Wedgwood Benn – journalist, radio producer; Wilson – academic, civil service; Bottomley – trade-union organizer; Callaghan – consultant to police federation; Crossman – journalist, academic; Jay – journalist, civil service; Marsh – trade-union official; Stewart– author, teacher.

Conservative. Barber – director, lawyer; du Cann – director of unit trusts; Hogg – barrister; Macleod – industry, journalist; Powell – director, academic; Robinson – insurance broker; Boyle – publisher; Heath – director; Home – party official; Maudling – director, lawyer; Rippon – barrister, director; Walker – insurance broker.

[5] Registrar-General's mid-year estimates 1966, UK population aged 21 years and over. (*Annual Abstract of Statistics*.)

[6] Elected in 1966. See D. Butler and A. King, *The British General Election of 1966* (Macmillan, 1967).

[7] Labour Government as at March 1967 (52 persons) and Conservative 'Leader's Committee' at March 1966 (14 persons).

Liberal. Hooson – barrister; Thorpe – barrister; Lubbock – engineer.

It is this similarity in background, especially in terms of education and occupation, that leads to the use of the term 'Establishment' with regard to British political leaders. This is taken to indicate, first, that the political leadership of this country has a homogeneous background (and that, in general, leaders of parties will be more like each other than like their followers or voters in this respect), and, second, that they are similar in these factors of background or 'life experience' to leaders from other important institutions of society – the commercial and financial world, the Civil Service, the Church, the Diplomatic Service, the armed forces, the traditional Universities and the independent professions. And, because of this, it is impossible to regard such leadership as representative, which means to some that it cannot be regarded as democratic either.

THE SELECTION PROCESS

All this assumes that the political decisions of party leaders are basically influenced by their personal histories. This in itself is, at the very least, 'not proven'. But such critics of British democratic leadership may be answered, if not completely satisfied, by reminding them of the procedures by which political leaders are selected.

Party leaders generally emerge from the ranks of Members of Parliament, who are themselves (*a*) elected in a fair and democratic manner by the citizenry, and (*b*) selected for candidature by local parties, who are under no compulsion to choose the stereotypes so commonly criticized today – Eton and Oxford, service in the Guards, directorships and a law practice. What factors account for the differences between the democratic theory and the unrepresentative results?

Ranney, whose book *Pathways to Parliament*[8] is an excellent analysis of many of the important factors involved in the selection process, emphasizes two points which are of interest in answering this question. In Britain, first, the headquarters of the parties rarely exercise their powers or their influence

[8] A. Ranney, *Pathways to Parliament.*

over the selection of candidates, except to refuse to sanction the very infrequent extremist or eccentric, or to press for the re-adoption of sitting Members in ill-favour with local officials (Mrs Braddock at Liverpool Exchange in 1955, and Elaine Burton at Coventry South, also in 1955, for example). This means, in consequence, that they cannot engineer a national balance between male and female candidates, young and old, graduates and early school-leavers, professional and manual occupations, Jews, Catholics, Protestants and atheists, etc. Since every local party wants its candidate to win, it tends to select the most attractive person as candidate, to appeal to the floating voters as well as the traditional party supporters. Thus one gets the well-spoken, well-educated male, preferably in an occupation which allows him ample time and sufficient income to nurse a constituency and fight an election. Second, selection is in effect the concern of the most active members of the local party, and since generally they have strong views on certain political issues, they are likely to allow these (quite legitimately, in their opinion) to influence their choice – and this may deny selection to certain types of otherwise quite suitable candidates.

A more recent book[9] has suggested that the concentration of the power of selection in the hands of only a very few local party officials is dangerous to democracy, since in perhaps two-thirds of the seats in any one Parliament this will be the equivalent of nominating the MP (remember, only fifty or so seats changed from one party to another in 1966, and the same number in 1964 – both considered to be large swings). The author therefore recommends the introduction of a type of American-style primary elections, whereby all party members could help to select the party's standard-bearer for the next election.

What actually takes place is this: persons who wish to be considered for candidates either indicate their willingness to a local party, or to Party Headquarters in London. In either case, Headquarters will wish to approve the final choice by the constituency. All three parties maintain lists, or 'panels', of names of people who wish to be chosen, with their personal details, information regarding their political experience, and

[9] P. Paterson, *The Selectorate* (MacGibbon & Kee, 1967).

their preference for certain areas or types of seat (e.g. urban constituencies, city suburbs, etc.). Since many of the most ambitious and attractive candidates are working in or near London, competition tends to decline (assuming seats of similar party strength in terms of shares of votes) as the distance from London increases. Labour's list is divided into two: the first list includes candidates who can obtain financial sponsorship, e.g. from a union.

Incumbent MPs – and, to a lesser extent, candidates – are usually offered unopposed selection for the following election if they wish. But assuming the incumbent does not wish to stand again, a local party wanting to select a candidate notifies Headquarters, and the local selection committee draws up a list of (*a*) names suggested by Headquarters, and (*b*) names it has received directly – perhaps including members, even officers, of the local party. Procedure then varies from place to place, but usually the process is as follows: by rejecting the obviously unsuitable, a first 'short-list' is obtained, and these dozen or twenty persons are interviewed (in an opposition-held seat, if it is safe, there may not be more than three or four names). Finally, a list of up to half-a-dozen or so of the likeliest candidates are asked to attend a selection conference.[10] This will be open to the General Management Committee in the case of the Constituency Labour Party, and to the Executive Committee in the case of the Conservatives. Usually a short speech and answers to questions, plus perhaps the likely suitability of Mrs Candidate, will determine whether a candidate is chosen or not. Only very rarely will the choice be a matter of controversy with Headquarters, who will not wish to appear as if they were restricting local party autonomy, and even less rarely will a formal veto from Headquarters be necessary.[11]

It is the selection process that gives most importance to the influence of local leaders on the party nationally, for it allows them to affect the representation of the party in Parliament, and, in some measure, to influence attitudes of Members towards their constituency party. The independent attitudes

[10] For an amusing fictional account of such a meeting, see David Walder's novel *The Short List* (Hutchinson, 1964).
[11] For examples of the use of the veto, see Ranney, *Pathways to Parliament*.

of Desmond Donnelly and Aneurin Bevan were supported by their local parties against pressures from the parliamentary leadership, yet over Suez, for example, Nigel Nicolson (the Conservative MP for Bournemouth East and Christchurch) and Stanley Evans (Labour MP for Wednesbury) both found that the constituency party, rather than the central leadership, was responsible for demanding their resignation from Parliament.

These local leaders are generally persons of some experience in the party, and possessed of sufficient enthusiasm to give up many hours per week to unpaid service in its cause. Apart from their influence in the selection process, they are important to party success in at least two other ways. They provide the bulk of conference delegates and conference resolutions, so their influence on the guidelines of over-all policy is not negligible (though it may not be appreciated by the national leadership), and it is the degree to which their enthusiasm carries over to others locally that may determine the success or failure of a marginal-seat campaign, of which Orpington (1962), Leyton (1965) and Hamilton (1967) are some of the more recent and spectacular by-election examples.

FOLLOWERS

From the point of view of the national leadership, such local officials are 'followers', though of a kind more committed to the party than the 'supporters', or the mass of electors who may give the party the minimum indication of sympathy, yet the most basic – the vote.

There are many ways of classifying the people who would give a positive answer to the question: 'Do you consider yourself to be a supporter of a political party?' Over a period of time, though, a three-fold division into *activists, supporters,* and *sympathizers* is useful, since it distinguishes between the three important types of resources that a political party requires in order to flourish. A *sympathizer* will be one of the 60–70 per cent of the electorate[12] who regard themselves as committed voters for one of the three main political parties,

[12] See the estimates in the study by J. Trenaman and D. McQuail, *Television and the Political Image* (Methuen, 1961), p. 128.

and will probably not consider depriving the party of his vote at least over a period of, say, three or four general elections. It is likely that such a person will, when necessary, be prepared to defend his choice in an argument, and possibly will contribute to party funds via the occasional raffle, jumble sale, or a collection at a political meeting. A *supporter* is rather more than this. He is prepared to become a member of a local party, at least if pressed. He may attend political meetings outside the period of an election campaign. He will take pains to vote at local, as well as general, elections. He might even take on duties of an occasional nature such as addressing envelopes or delivering leaflets. Whereas the main resource offered by the sympathizer is the *vote*, the supporter offers *financial aid* in addition, through his membership subscription, other contributions, and by sometimes performing tasks which would otherwise have to be paid for, or not be carried out at all. The *activist*, along with his vote and his financial aid, offers *time and political experience.* He is prepared – indeed, is often eager – to stand for office, and to accept responsibilities as Chairman, Secretary, Press Officer, Treasurer or (where a professional agent is not available) as electoral agent. Many activists offer a long political experience to the party, giving up holidays to attend the Annual Conference or organize the local or general election campaign. They are almost invariably interested in, and knowledgeable about, areas of national and local policy, and can be of the greatest assistance to the local candidate, councillor, or Member of Parliament.

The rewards for being a follower in any of these three degrees are related to the functions of political parties which were discussed in the preceding chapter; and, like these functions, the rewards may be classed as formal or latent – i.e. those satisfactions which are consciously related to the purposes of party activity, and those that accrue, as it were, indirectly or accidentally.

For the voter, the rewards include the sense of participation in a civic process, and the fulfilment of a civic duty. More likely, for voters who regard themselves as 'sympathizers', they will involve a sense of partisanship that can range from supporting one's traditional loyalty, all the way to an expression of class-consciousness and class-hatred. Although the single vote of one elector rarely makes the difference between victory and defeat, or saves a lost deposit, it does allow the voter to experience involvement in the political process, and this can be regarded as rewarding in itself.[13]

The rewards to a supporter, in addition, may include a greater sense of 'citizen competence'[14] which comes from the greater degree of involvement in the election. There is generally a personal expression of gratitude from the candidate or party chairman for work done, or for money subscribed. There is the feeling that, as a supporter, a person has more right to express an opinion and to criticize party policy or strategy. Social mobility may also be involved – support may lead to activism, and both may confer status that otherwise might not be available.

The rewards to the activist are all these and more. He has responsibility as well as involvement. Politics becomes more than a partly-social interest, it becomes second only to his occupation in terms of time, effort and attention. The party's successes become his successes, its failures are taken as, in some measure, personal failure. The ultimate reward for some activists is to make the transition from being a follower to becoming a leader – by election to the local council, for instance, for community leaders, or to Parliament and on to higher office.

Most followers join political parties by invitation, except for the very enthusiastic partisan who seeks out party headquarters and joins in this way. Some become party members through joining the associated Club first. Some join the local Labour Party through trade union channels. The influence of University life, with its political societies and its opportunities for political activity is a strong inducement for graduates to join the party. The ancillary youth groups are another route to membership.

[13] For a further discussion of the functions and rewards of voting, see R. Rose and H. Mossawir, 'Voting and Elections: A Functional Analysis', *Political Studies*, June 1967.

[14] A term employed in G. Almond and S. Verba, *The Civic Culture* (Princeton, 1963), to indicate the notion of citizen influence over the formation of policy.

THE INTERNAL POLITICS OF BRITISH PARTIES

The relationship between leaders and followers is of great importance in the study of political parties. In particular, the question of the degree of democracy within the parties must be raised: since there is some agreement that political parties, by competing for office and power within a democracy, aid the democratic process, are their own organizations also deserving of the name 'democratic'?

The best statement to the contrary was produced by Robert Michels; his 'iron law of oligarchy' has long been regarded as the classic indictment of the organization of democratic political parties. Michels claimed that his studies of political parties (mainly European socialist parties) had demonstrated conclusively that, however democratic in intention might be the constitutional arrangements of political parties, inevitably in a large-scale organization power gravitates into the hands of a few. Decisions have to be taken, policies executed, appointments to office have to be made, money has to be spent, and so on. These tasks clearly cannot always be performed by a full meeting of a mass party, or by postal voting, or by representative assemblies of the party. With these powers goes the power of leadership itself, and this enables the party elite to perpetuate itself in office.

The rest of this chapter will be concerned with seeing how far such a diagnosis applies to British parties, with reference to four key elements of power-relations: the appointment and change of Leaders, the distribution of power within the party, the way in which decisions are made, and the sources and control of finance.

Leadership changes. How are party Leaders (and thus potential Premiers) chosen? In all three parties, the basic procedures are now very similar: the members of the parliamentary party vote, on a second-ballot system if necessary. Until 1965, in the Conservative Party the Leader was selected by means of several elder statesmen of the party taking 'soundings'. He was not elected, he emerged. However, mindful perhaps of the dissatisfaction over the method (and perhaps also over the result) of his own emergence, Sir Alec Douglas-Home instituted, on party advice, a method of election which was later used to choose his own successor. The Liberals had no call to use a method of choice until 1967, since other Leaders had been almost self-selecting, or at least were chosen, without much opposition, by the retiring Leader. A brief description, then, of the most recent election in each party will illustrate the actual procedures used.

The death of Hugh Gaitskell in 1963, still quite young to be a party Leader (he was 56), left the Labour Party without an obvious successor, though Harold Wilson (who had been the youngest member of Attlee's administration when he was 31), George Brown (Gaitskell's deputy Leader, and supported by the right-wing and some of the more orthodox of the trades unions) and James Callaghan (Gaitskell's Shadow Chancellor) all accepted nomination. The first ballot gave Wilson an unexpectedly high vote of 115 of the 244 votes cast (i.e. about 47 per cent), while Brown polled 88 votes (about 36 per cent) and Callaghan 41 (about 17 per cent). Under the rules, as no candidate had 50 per cent plus one of the votes cast, a second election was necessary, with only the first two candidates allowed on the ballot-paper. This increased Wilson's vote to 144 (about 58 per cent) while Brown increased to 103 (about 42 per cent).

Although he had revived the fortunes of his party to the point where the expected defeat of 1964 was almost averted, Sir Alec Douglas-Home's leadership of the Conservative Party had been the subject of intermittent criticism ever since his recommendation by Macmillan to the Queen in 1963. He had regarded himself as a temporary Leader, until a clear successor emerged. By 1965, he was apparently satisfied that, if not one, then two likely successors were available, and established in the Party. The result of an inquiry, conducted by Lord Blakenham, the Chairman of the Party, into the institution of a new method of selecting the Leader, had been accepted by Sir Alec in February 1965, and this made his departure easier, for at least the quarrels that had marred his own first months of office would not be repeated for his successor. He resigned in July 1965, and the new electoral methods went into action, uneventfully, and with little or no controversy. Three candidates offered themselves: Edward Heath, strongly associated with the pro-Common Market sections of the Party, and an ex-Chief Whip, with considerable ministerial experience under Macmillan and Home; Reginald Maudling, who had been tipped by some as a possible successor to Macmillan, and who had acted as Home's Chancellor of the Exchequer; and Enoch Powell, also an experienced Minister, regarded with most favour by the right-wing and free enterprise sections of the Party. To win on the first ballot, a candidate had to fulfil two requirements: he had to receive an absolute majority of the votes cast, and also be ahead of his nearest rival by a margin of 15 per cent of the votes cast. Should either of these conditions not be met, a second ballot, with new nominations possible, would be held, requiring only an absolute majority for victory. Failing this, a third ballot, with first and second preferences indicated, and limited to the first three candidates on the second ballot, would provide a winner, if necessary by re-allocation of second preferences of the candidate with the least first preferences. Though the system was a trifle complicated to the layman, it emphasized just that search for consensus that had guided the choice of Macmillan and other party leaders in the search for a successor in 1963.

On this occasion the complications were not required. The voting on the first ballot was: Heath 150 (51 per cent); Maudling 133 (44 per cent); Powell 15 (5 per cent). Although lacking the 15 per cent margin necessary, Heath became Leader once it was known that no other candidate had presented nomination papers for the second ballot. Maudling had conceded victory to Heath once the result was known by immediately declining renomination, and this discouraged any other candidate from making a divisive second ballot necessary.

Jo Grimond had been associated with the image of the Liberal Party in most people's minds for so long that his announcement of resignation in January 1967 came as a bigger shock than any such resignation this century. He, too, felt that the Party had a successor able to take over, now that Labour seemed entrenched in office for a further four years or so. Again a method of balloting was used, as provided by the Party Constitution, though with the alternative vote used instead of the second ballot (this, in effect, combined the first and the second ballot in one operation). The three candidates were, Jeremy Thorpe, the Treasurer of the Party; Eric

Lubbock, victor of Orpington and Party Whip; and Emlyn Hooson, who represented Montgomery, seat of Grimond's predecessor in the leadership, Clement Davies. The voting of the small Liberal parliamentary representation was: Thorpe, 6 votes; Hooson and Lubbock, 3 votes each. Though Thorpe was short of an absolute majority, the alternative preferences of the two second-place candidates could hardly be re-allocated and the situation was resolved by each agreeing to stand down in favour of Thorpe.

The distribution of power. In the preceding chapter, a description of the various institutions within political parties was offered. The question of how 'power' of various kinds was distributed among these institutions was not given emphasis. Three statements can be made at the outset that bear on this question:

(i) In both major parties, the Leader has sufficient power available to carry through almost any decision, provided that it is not too far from the expectations of his ministerial colleagues (or their equivalents) – and he influences their selection in any case; of course, this depends on the Party having no ready replacement for him, but if it has such a replacement, compromise over policy is unlikely to delay the challenge for long.

(ii) There are substantial formal (or 'constitutional') differences between the powers of subsidiary elements of the two main parties, and these formal differences are of importance in many matters, such as the retention of Clause IV in the Labour Party Constitution, the influence of trades unions at constituency, parliamentary, and national levels of the Labour Party, and the different sensitivities of Labour and Conservative rank-and-file to 'inner-party democracy'.

(iii) Whereas it can be argued that: 'throughout its disordered 1950s, Labour continued to display its lack of a true elite and its obsessive commitment to intraparty democracy',[15] it can also be argued that the accession of Harold Wilson to the Leadership of the Party, and its five very full years of governmental office, have lessened considerably the force of this criticism.

Both parties recognize that communication within the party

[15] S. Beer, *Modern British Politics* (Faber, 1965), p. 388.

is important, but opinion can be influential without being powerful. Both parties accept their role as elements of a democratic political system, but this does not necessarily commit them to the emulation of such a democratic system within their own organizations.

Thus, in summary, the distribution of power within the parties can be stated as follows: in the Labour Party, ultimate formal power lies with the Annual Conference, considerable delegated discretionary power with the National Executive Committee, a certain amount of power over policy and the power to select the leadership (including the elected committee of the Parliamentary Party) with the MPs, and the autonomy of the constituency party – within a more rigid set of rules than applies to the Conservatives – is accepted on local matters. But Labour now has a strong, forceful Leader in Harold Wilson, and the precedents of power which he creates, like those belonging to the offices of Prime Minister or President of the USA, are likely to possess the 'ratchet effect' of being available to his successors, who may add to them, but will not be able easily to lessen or ignore them. It can also be argued that Labour now possesses an elite, experienced in office, who, with Wilson, have abandoned any 'obsessive commitment to intraparty democracy' that may have existed before. The channels of party influence are open from ward to constituency to region to Conference, but more than ever the discretionary, day-to-day powers of the leadership are paramount. Devaluation, immigration restrictions, foreign affairs, incomes policy – all these important areas of decision-making can find little or no warrant in decisions of party representative bodies, except, as with incomes policy, post facto.

In the Conservative Party it is history, rather than the Conference or any similar body, that is the source of basic principles, and there is far less demand for the partition of authority among party institutions. Randolph Churchill's attempt in 1883–4 to give the representative assembly of the Party authority over matters of policy failed at least as much because this was considered alien to the party ethos, as because it challenged the authority of Salisbury and the parliamentary leadership. The local party is even more powerful, in most respects, than in the Labour Party, and it is the Conservative leadership, from Butler in the 1940s, to Lord Carrington, Selwyn Lloyd, and Edward Heath in the 1960s, who have stressed the two-way flow of internal party communication, rather than the Labour Party. But the Party is an instrument, rather than a 'movement', and overemphasis on democracy for its own sake, at constituency, parliamentary or national level, has never attracted the attentions of the Conservative faithful.

Decision-making procedures. If any single phenomenon of party development can be selected as representing the postwar change in the power-structures of political parties, it is the greater attention paid by all parties to using the machinery of representation for improving the making of decisions in the party, and their acceptance by the membership. While it is true that, in imitation of Churchill's use of Lindemann, and the American practices of Roosevelt, Kennedy and Johnson, experts are used to a greater extent at national level (e.g. Professor Kaldor, Thomas Balogh, Sir Solly Zuckerman, Professor Beloff, Michael Fogarty), constituencies are encouraged to consider political problems and submit their views to Headquarters.[16] The leadership itself uses policy panels of party authorities from time to time, such as the Liberals' local government group, the Labour publicity and advertising group,[17] and the Conservative groups set up under Mr Heath in 1964,[18] while the use of parliamentary groups is on the increase, especially in view of the likely increase in House of Commons Committees of a functional nature.

Finance. 'I should like all the finances of the Tory Party to be open for inspection for anyone who may wish to look at them, be he friend or foe. Where you allow secret expenditure, you will certainly have corrupt expenditure.' (Randolph Churchill, 1883).[19] Until very recently, little was known about sources of party finance, but recent studies[20] have thrown

[16] E.g. the Conservative Party's 'Three-Way Contact' series, for discussion and report back on various topics.
[17] See R. Rose, *Influencing Voters* (Faber, 1967), p. 72.
[18] See D. Butler and A. King, *Election of 1966*, p. 60.
[19] Quoted in I. Bulmer-Thomas, *The Growth of the British Party System*, vol. I (John Baker, 1965), p. 130.
[20] E.g. the appendix in Rose, *Influencing Voters*, M. Harrison, *Trade Unions and the Labour Party since 1945* (Allen & Unwin, 1960), and the studies of the 1964 and 1966 elections by Butler and King.

more light on this matter, and in January 1968 the Conservatives published for the first time a breakdown of its central income and expenditure. Finance is important in relation to party democracy for at least these three reasons:

(i) To the extent that it is provided by the membership, this is an indicator of the degree of commitment and involvement felt by the rank-and-file.

(ii) 'Who pays the piper . . .' – if it is suspected that much comes from non-party contributors, this leads to the fear of obligation to, and even control by, such contributors, e.g. the trades unions or the industrial combines.

(iii) The method by which financial expenditure is controlled indicates the extent of oligarchic, rather than democratic, procedures of party control.

The estimates of income and expenditure given by the Conservatives for the financial year 1966–7 showed a central income of £642,000 and an expenditure of £1,085,000. Donations (from individuals and corporate bodies such as companies) amounted to £501,000, of which an estimated[21] £400,000 came from industry. Constituencies paid £204,000 to Headquarters, and income from investments was £21,000. The Party had reserves of £796,000.

Labour Party income is heavily dependent on the 'political levy' paid by most members of affiliated trades unions. In the mid-1960s this was running at nearly £100,000 per year. Dues from constituency members only provide a minor proportion of party income, and considerable reliance has been placed on other fund-raising activities such as weekly lotteries. Investment income for Headquarters is about £15,000, and miscellaneous receipts about £8,000. In election year, extra finance is received from donations – nearly £70,000 in 1964.

Liberal Party income comes from constituency party quotas (about £15,000 yearly) and donations (about £50,000 on average each year), while certain sums are available from various trusts and bequests. Certainly the total is under £100,000 in most years.

With regard to the three points raised above, it would appear that the Liberal and Labour parties, in their reliance on widespread contributions from members and supporters,

[21] *Daily Telegraph*, 5 January 1968.

can claim in this respect to be more 'democratic' than the Conservatives, but certainly the Conservative Party is increasing its emphasis on small, but widespread, contributions, for at least two reasons, not directly concerned with democratic practices as such. It fears that industrial and other large donations may be less fruitful than before, if only because of the need for disclosure of such contributions in company balance-sheets since Labour's election victory in 1966, and it realizes that the gathering of small, regular subscriptions serves a propaganda purpose as well, maintaining contact with the rank-and-file, and stimulating party workers to get out on to the doorstep.

The Labour Party's reliance on trade-union levies can be questioned as to its relation to democracy, in view of the need to contract-out by those who wish to avoid this payment in the unions which have voted to affiliate. At present, 20 per cent contract out, but it is estimated that as many as 50 per cent would not pay if it was necessary to contract-in. This would cut party income from this source by as much as 7s 6d in the £, or nearly £40,000 per year.

Neither Conservative nor Labour governments can be accused of pandering too obviously to their main sources of finance – business and the unions. Mr Wilson's speeches on incomes policy, Conservative legislation against monopolies, and the insistence of governments of both parties on the need for certain types of government economic regulation can be cited as evidence of that. But equally both parties can be assumed to be mindful of their financial reliance on these interests, and to this extent the rank-and-file have rivals for influence over the shaping of party policy.

All three parties are now to publish their accounts, but disclosure will only point up the degree of control available to the leadership and Party Headquarters, through control over finance. This has been a continual source of contention in the Liberal Party especially, for the local parties have claimed that they should be allowed to spend the money they raise locally – most local parties have little or no surplus anyway. They say that money raised is an indicator of support, so it is best to use it to build up further support in a favourable location, rather than allow Headquarters to use it for deposits for hopeless candidatures. This is countered by the leadership's claim that local support is often more influenced by *national* strength, *national* publicity, and a *national* spread of candidatures than by local efforts, and that money is better spent on a co-ordinated national campaign. Such an argument can be found, of course, from time to time in the other parties.

Conclusion. The selection of the Leader, the distribution of power, the procedures for decision-making, and control of finance, all point to the same conclusion: in all three British parties, effective control is, and to a large extent inevitably must be, concentrated in a few hands – generally the Leader, the chief members of the parliamentary party, and a small number of top executives in the central bureaucracy (including, for Labour, important trade-union leaders such as George Woodcock and Frank Cousins). The rank-and-file members, the constituency leaders, the representative organs of the parties, the associated interest-groups, all have influence which varies in its importance with the circumstances – the proximity of an election, the role of the party in Parliament (whether in power or opposition, for instance), the questions under consideration, and so forth.

Are the parties then undemocratic? This is a difficult question, which depends for its answer on what one measures democracy by. But, since the supersession of Athenian or New England direct democracy, representation, bureaucratic management, and the necessary responsibilities of leadership all limit the possibilities today of any national organization living up to the standards of strict democracy in terms of broad-based power distribution. Nonetheless, the parties in Britain play an essential part in maintaining democratic politics within their own organizations and within the state as a whole. However, other organized groups also have a part to play, and attention must now be given to the organization and influence of pressure-groups, lobbies and interests in British politics.

5 Pressure-groups

Political parties in British politics tend to be clearly-defined institutions with quite sophisticated forms of organization, and, as was shown in Chapter 2, their purposes are directly concerned with politics. Pressure-groups and similar non-party groups which are concerned for at least some of the time with political influence, are, on the other hand, not so readily-defined, vary greatly in their degree and style of political influence, as well as organization, and their political activities may be regarded by them as of the highest importance, or, on the contrary, of no more than marginal significance relative to their other purposes.

Because of some of the more lurid exposures of the concealed influence of pressure-groups on political decisions over the past hundred years, especially in American politics, the term has acquired unsavoury overtones, as has a similar word: lobby. The words interest and interest-group are also not free from such taint, at least for those whose philosophy of politics inclines them either towards the acceptance of an atomistic individualism as the proper organizational basis for society, or the postulation of a general will, be it of the Rousseauean, Burkean, or totalitarian variety. Yet, in attempting to describe and analyse the workings of the British political process, it is impossible to ignore the extent to which it relies on non-party groups, and it is almost equally difficult to avoid employment of the terms lobby, pressure-group and interest.

The distinctions between these terms can be stated thus: a lobby is organized and operates solely for purposes of political influence on a particular matter, e.g. the Rhodesian lobby, or the road-haulage lobby; a pressure-group has political functions alongside its other functions, e.g. the TUC, the AA, or the League against Cruel Sports; interests are the common factors which may link various individuals (or organizations) together into interest-groups, which may then from time to time find it necessary to involve themselves in political activity as a lobby or a pressure-group – e.g. the motoring interest, the press interest, or the interests concerned with the preservation of historic buildings.

RECENT GROUP ACTIVITY

Some of these distinctions can be illustrated by an over-view of some recent interventions in British politics by various groups. In one way, the most spectacular, yet the least effective, have been the series of vaguely left-wing movements which have ranged from the Campaign for Nuclear Disarmament to the anti Viet-Nam War campaign. These 'movements' have employed the tactics of the lobby, and indeed have won over several Members of Parliament to their side, though perhaps less in a concern for the political importance of the MP in Parliament (given the diminution of the power of the back-bencher since the war) than to serve as prominent patrons along with assorted actresses, philosophers, playwrights and academics for purposes of publicity or respectability. They have acted as interest-groups in that they have brought together the rather wide range of individuals with views (in CND) extending from uncompromising pacifism to those who believe that, though war may be an unavoidable condition of international society, nuclear war would be disastrous, and hence nuclear weapons must be abandoned, even unilaterally. In the recent anti Viet-Nam War demonstrations, the additional ingredients of pro-Communism and anti-Americanism were present, along with the vaguer near-anarchism of the student power movements. And, of course, these movements have tried to be pressure-groups through employment of a wide range of tactics aimed at altering policy, from sit-downs and marches to organized abstention at elections, parliamentary candidatures, civil disobedience, letters from prominents in the quality press, and questions to candidates at election time.

The activity of the Ministry of Transport, under the Labour Government especially, in such matters as the introduction of the 70 m.p.h. speed limit, breathalyser tests for drivers suspected of being intoxicated, and the Transport Bill intended to apportion more efficiently goods traffic between road and rail haulage, has led to a corresponding increase in the political interventions of various groups concerned with the motorist or the road-haulage industry. Whereas the speed limit and the breathalyser tests stimulated the efforts of only the motorists' organizations (and, in the case of the drink-and-driving laws, the not unexpected opposition of the brewing and licensed premises' interests), the opposition to the Transport Bill has been encouraged by the announced policies of the Conservative leadership, and this has added considerable force – as well as organizational resources – to the campaign. Letters to the press, constituents' pressure on Members of Parliament, advertisements, demonstrations, questions in the House of Commons, and parliamentary attacks on the legislation itself have all been combined in this campaign. It is thus a good example of an issue which has prompted party and group hostilities.

A more formal series of opportunities for group influence arose with the recent inquiries into the Civil Service, local government, trade-unions and employers' associations, and the future of the independent schools. With such commissions or committees of inquiry, it is the practice to invite interested bodies to submit evidence, and the extent to which this invitation is accepted can be gauged from the list at the end of the published report of witnesses giving oral or written evidence. Thus, among the bodies giving evidence to the Fulton Committee on the Civil Service was the Treasury (as, in one respect, the 'manager' of the Civil Service) and the various associations of civil servants; the inquiry into trades unions and employers' associations has taken evidence from the Ministries of Labour and Social Security, as well as from the Confederation of British Industry, the TUC and the Fabian Society; the commission examining the independent schools has heard from the National Union of Teachers, the Comprehensive Schools Committee, the Incorporated Association of Preparatory Schools, the TUC, the National Secular Society and the Workers' Educational Association, among others; and the following list represents some of the many organizations (apart from various local authorities and the Ministry of Housing and Local Government) who have given evidence to the Maud Commission on Local Government in England and Wales: Architectural Association; Association of Councillors;

Association of Municipal Corporations; Confederation of British Industry; Corporation of Secretaries; Department of Economic Affairs; Electoral Reform Society; Institute of Journalists; Institute of Local Government Administrators; Institute of Municipal Engineers; Liberal Party; National Association of Local Government Officers; National Union of Teachers; Rural District Councils Association; Society of Town Clerks; Town Planning Institute; Trades Union Congress; University of Manchester. Though such formal, almost judicial, presentation of evidence in a reasoned manner is far removed from the popular notion of semi-illicit pressures associated with the idea of group influence, it is an important aspect of British policy making, and, given the spirit of British democratic politics, is often more influential than cruder measures could ever hope to be.

A less broad-ranging case, yet one which well typifies the reactions of British citizens to policies they feel are hastily conceived or harmful to the rights of the individual, is the Stansted affair. The proposal to make Stansted the site of London's third major airport brought strong reactions from various groups whose interests were threatened by the scheme: farmers who would lose valuable agricultural land, residents whose domestic amenities would suffer, or be destroyed altogether by the expanded runways, local councils, proponents of alternative sites, and so on. They raised funds, formed a fighting group, and opposed the measure through the various stages of inquiry and ministerial action. They presented evidence showing how much better other sites such as Foulness would be, and tried to enlist public opinion and parliamentary support to their cause. All seemed in vain, as the Government reaffirmed its decision, but victory was won when at last the announcement of a new and more thorough inquiry was made in early 1968, and in 1969 a new list of alternative sites omitted Stansted altogether.

THE HISTORY OF GROUP INFLUENCE IN BRITISH POLITICS

It is more difficult to put a date to the commencement of group influence in British politics than it is to indicate the start of party politics. Unlike parties, groups have not depended on the existence of Parliament for their activities, and a number of recognizable groups existed in British politics before the days of Parliament and party – the Church, the boroughs, the merchant guilds, the City of London, and so on. But, as with the parties, their story is tangled up to a great extent with the dynastic and religious conflicts of our early history.

By the start of the eighteenth century, a more settled pattern of groups and interests is observable. Various social interests can be discerned: sects, for instance, such as the Quakers, groups of 'foreign' inhabitants such as the Jews and the Huguenots, and, at least by the end of the century, certain humanitarian groups such as those opposed to the slave trade. Economic groups were important, among them the East India Company, and the Russian traders, the money interests of the City of London, the coach and canal transport interests, and various groups of manufacturers such as the metal traders of Birmingham, the textile manufacturers of Lancashire and Yorkshire, the North Staffordshire potters, and so forth. It is important to note the strong regional basis of such organizations. Nationally organized groups came later. They were concerned with local problems, though these might have been affected by national policies, and looked to their local representatives to press their case – similar to the local basis of much of the Congressional politics of the USA even today. Ad hoc groups also existed, over parliamentary reform, for instance, such as the Yorkshire Association. All these groups were concerned from time to time with the possibility of political action to obtain desired changes in policy.

The development of a national economy with the progress of the industrial revolution led to a need for groups to be organized on a national scale. The growth of a London-based national press, developments in cheap printing, and, especially, the creation of a nation-wide network of railways all aided the process. But economic problems also became much more associated with political developments, and the growth of parties, the reform of Parliament and local government, the increase in the participation of the middle-classes in the political process were all of importance.

Thus the politics of the nineteenth century became as much

the politics of groups as the politics of parties. Loyalties to class, occupation and interest were often stronger than loyalties to party, and the sanctions could be stronger, as MPs for agricultural constituencies were well aware when faced with Sir Robert Peel's 'betrayal' over repeal of the Corn Laws, for example. The economic and political philosophies of the period permitted an emphasis on interest as a guiding principle for political choice, though, in Parliament at least, such interest had to be overt, not concealed, and was subject to various procedural limitations such as restrictions on the right to sit on committees or to vote where such interests were involved.

Examples of interests, pressure-groups and lobbies from the nineteenth century abound. Factory reform led to a parliamentary alliance of the working-classes of the industrial north, reforming radicals and the 'agricultural' Tories, anxious to be avenged on the factory-owners of the Whig Party for the repeal of the Corn Laws. Whether one reads a history of the factory movement,[1] a life of Shaftesbury, or the 'Blue Books' on factory conditions the same impressions of interests, organization and political pressure can be obtained. Chartism and the Anti-Corn Law League were two of the most famous non-party political groups of modern history, even though in the short-term, the first failed and the other succeeded. Their histories bring out the importance of leadership, organization, a strong financial base, and the advantages of a clearly defined, limited policy if a group is to be successful.

The development of trade-unions is a chapter in itself in any history of group politics in the nineteenth century. It typifies the development of national organizations which grew from local or regional roots. Not until 1868 was there a Trades Union Congress, but for fifty or sixty years before that trade-unions had been concerned with political matters – legislative restrictions on the right to organize, the political emancipation of the (skilled) working-class, Poor Law and factory reform and many other measures.

Groups concerned with non-economic matters also developed – groups for the reform or the defence of religious positions, groups interested in Irish or Bulgarian or Imperial matters, groups pressing for educational or Civil Service or sanitary

[1] E.g., J. Ward, *The Factory Movement* (Macmillan, 1962).

improvement, groups wishing to further the cause of women's votes, birth control, stricter Sabbatarian observance, or temperance. But of all these groups, whether economic or non-economic in purpose, one of the most interesting was one particularly associated with the nineteenth century itself: the railway interest, and a more detailed examination of the way in which this unorganized interest developed into a highly organized pressure-group by the end of the century will illustrate many of the features of group politics in the nineteenth century.

From the very beginning of railway construction in Britain, promoters were faced with the challenge of opposition which had to be met within the political arena, for each railway project required a private Bill in Parliament to be passed which allowed it to buy land, bridge rivers, raise capital, etc., in order to proceed with the line. Opponents – individual and corporate – included landowners whose properties lay on the route, and who could be forced to sell for a judicially determined price if the Bill passed, canal owners and stage-coach operators, who would probably be injured financially by railway competition, public schools such as Eton, fearful of the moral effects of a nearby railway on their pupils, and later other railways, who wished to defeat competitive lines. The companies met this type of opposition as it arose, but in doing so developed the political skills, contacts and procedures which later were to be employed profitably in contests over more general political matters, such as safety regulations, government control over rates, the right to combine with other companies, etc.

By the time the government had decided to impose some general regulations on the railway industry in 1844, the companies had three very important weapons to hand– they had a small but effective group of railway directors sitting in the House of Commons itself (some elected as directors, others offered directorships because they were already Members of Parliament), they decided to proceed from interest to pressure-group by organizing a representative body of directors and managers to handle opposition to Gladstone's Bill, and they could call on the services of experienced 'parliamentary agents' – skilled in opposition to private railway Bills – to lobby MPs and direct a parliamentary opposition against the Bill. Evidence against the proposals of the government was offered to the Select Committee which was considering the question of state regulation of the new industry of railways, arguments against it were supplied to the press, speakers made well-briefed orations against it in Parliament, and Members of Parliament were provided with ample administrative, political and electoral reasons why the Bill should be defeated. The effect was that Gladstone's Bill had its more radical proposals modified, and aspects such as provision for state purchase of companies were watered down so that they achieved practically nothing.

The interest of the railway companies in preserving their commercial freedom continued to provide a basis for organization from time to time, and, in 1867, a permanent Railway Companies' Association was at last founded, which remained in existence as spokesman for the industry until nationalization. Parliamentary representation grew, until by 1866 there were some 146 directors of railway companies in the Commons.

RAILWAY DIRECTORS IN THE HOUSE OF COMMONS[2]

Year	MP-Directors	No. of directorships held
1840	19	21
1845	30	41
1850	68	92
1855	98	144
1860	110	178
1865	142	235

By the end of the century, national organization of interests had become a much more common feature of political life. The railways faced concerted attacks from organizations of traders and users of railway facilities, from groups promoting policies of railway nationalization, from trade unions, and so forth. The sophistication of national party organization was matched by the increasing complexity of national groups and

[2] G. K. Roberts, *The development of a railway interest, and its relation to Parliament, 1830–1868* (unpublished Ph.D. thesis, University of London, 1965), p. 144.

national interests; at the turn of the century a list of groups could have included many organizations like the following twenty examples: Association of Municipal Corporations; British Medical Association; British National Temperance League; Chartered Institute of Secretaries; Co-operative Wholesale Society; County Councils Association; Headmasters' Conference; Institute of Bankers; Institute of Builders; Institute of Chartered Accountants; Institute of Journalists; Land Nationalization Society; Law Society; National Secular Society; National Union of Teachers; National Union of Women's Suffrage Societies; Railway Companies Association; Royal Society for the Prevention of Cruelty to Animals; Shipping Federation; Trades Union Congress.

In addition, there were numerous trade-unions and employers' associations.

The present century has seen two very important developments in attitudes towards groups in politics – they have been accepted by many people as being in some way important to democracy, and they have been recognized as belonging to a particular form of political society, the pluralist industrial polity. A later chapter gives further consideration to both these points in relation to other states and other times, but it is sufficient here to note the importance of group activity in developed political societies throughout the western world, their role in developing states in Africa, Asia and Latin America (i.e. where groups are able to develop, and where they have opportunities for political action, the regime seems to have a better chance of avoiding instability or dictatorship), and the way in which totalitarianisms of the Left (as in China or the USSR) and of the Right (Czarist Russia, Hitler's Germany) give priority to the elimination or assimilation of all groups outside party control.

Whether coincidence or not – and one cannot explain away all the associations between these developments as coincidence – the maturity of British democracy in the period from the end of the First World War to the Representation of the People Act 1948 occurred at the same time as groups multiplied on a national scale, and came to be accepted as necessary adjuncts to maintaining in a complex economy some degree of informed, popular-based control.

Trade-unions, among the most influential group organizations of the modern period, had become nationally organized for the most part, and a process of amalgamation made them larger in size, yet fewer in number. A similar, if less obvious, process occurred with employers' associations, so that national industrywide negotiations were facilitated. In some cases, as with Whitley Councils, the teachers' negotiating committees, and some industrial groups, the state became a 'third partner' in such matters. Nationalization after the Second World War meant that, in a very real sense, the state *was* the employer (if, on occasion, an employer with divided and conflicting views of the facts of economic life!).

The General Strike (1926) was a dangerous, but in some sense a valuable experience for the British political system, in that it set fairly clear limits to the political powers of trade-unions as pressure-groups. Given a fairly free hand in economic negotiations (at least, prior to the Prices and Incomes policy of the Wilson Government), the unions and the TUC received clear warning in 1926 that once a subject under negotiation became 'political' to an important degree, the government could not abdicate its responsibilities for the safety of the state or the protection of its citizens and their property, and the proper institutions to decide on political matters were the elected Parliament and a government which could command the confidence of Parliament. This is not to be uncritical of the causes or the consequences of the strike itself, but to recognize that – like the Civil War in America, or the student riots in West Germany and France in 1968 – irrespective of the *issues* involved, a challenge to the decision-making authority of the state must be met by exerting the utmost coercive power of the state if this becomes necessary for the survival of the authority of the regime. It is not fanciful to suppose that many of the more responsible trade-union leaders in 1926 also appreciated this, and were thankful not to have their demands accepted as a result of such a challenge to the state, whatever their sympathies might have been with regard to the miners' case, which had precipitated the General Strike.

With the more complex economy came a more complex society in the twentieth century. Two world wars made the problem of veteran care and pensions an issue of some importance (though never to the degree to which the USA experienced veterans' pressure), and various organizations such as the British Legion and the British Limbless Ex-Servicemen's Association became of political consequence.[3] The coming of the motor-car led to the formation of the Automobile Association and the Royal Automobile Club – and any Minister of Transport will appreciate the pressures *they* can exert whenever legislation concerning motorists is under consideration, be it a new safety regulation, more tax on petrol or vehicles, or a cut in the programme of motorway construction. A kind of Parkinson's Law applies in agriculture – and again a parallel with the USA can be noted – whereby a decline in farm employment nevertheless leads to an increase in the influence of the agrarian interest on political decisions, as, for instance, measured by the growth of subsidies and other public payments to farmers. Credit for this goes chiefly to an ever-stronger National Farmers' Union. Groups concerned with civil liberties, race relations, nuclear disarmament, the Territorial Army, civil defence, the abolition of blood sports or the promotion of field sports, Sabbatarian observance or the 'brighter Sunday', the preservation of historic buildings, or of footpaths in the countryside, or of independent educational institutions can all be found in post-war politics. Interests, too, though not necessarily organized, are of influence. This can be seen by the attention paid to them (at least verbally) by Members of Parliament and party spokesmen – youth, old age pensioners, commuters, office-workers, mortgage payers, consumers, sportsmen, shareholders, immigrants, parents, pedestrians, and so forth.

The recognition of 'interests' as having a legitimate right to influence the making of decisions (but not to make them themselves) is one of the noticeable lessons which contemporary politicians have learned from the history of twentieth century group action. It is necessary, for legislation which was not based on the consultation of affected groups has so often proved to be difficult or impossible to implement. It is wise, for much modern legislation, though based on a simple and

[3] See the case-study by G. Wootton, *The Politics of Influence* (Routledge & Kegan Paul, 1963).

straightforward policy (safety in factories, differential taxation of employment in 'service' and in 'manufacturing' firms, alterations in the law concerning abortion, a new earnings-based pensions policy), requires consideration of complex factors of a technical nature, and often only private groups can provide the information, statistics, and expert advice needed on such matters. It is non-partisan, for what is remarkable since the end of the last war is the impossibility of a Labour government ignoring all interests except those of the unions, or a Conservative government failing to consult with the 'class enemy', organized labour. And it is democratic, to some extent anyway, for the Government–Opposition debate is made more informative to the public by the interjection of group opinion, either externally or through parliamentary spokesmen. Contemporary politics has been termed 'mass politics' and 'consensual politics', but it is very much 'group politics' as well.

THE PRESENT SITUATION

It would be almost impossible to list all the groups which may from time to time take part in political activity, if only because new groups are continually being formed, others disappear, while others take up a concern with politics for the first time. Obviously some groups are sufficiently important and so well-known that they cannot escape mention in referring to the contemporary situation, and this will be done, but first, in order to understand the differences between various types of groups with reference to their degree of concern with political matters, the following classificatory scheme can be used for guidance.

Already it has been suggested that there is a useful distinction to be drawn between lobbies, pressure-groups, and interests (above, p. 78). Three other dimensions can now be added, which aid our appreciation of how and why groups concern themselves with politics. First there is the question of whether the group is permanently established, with a continuing regard for certain on-going problems such as the interests of motorists (the AA) or of trade unions (the TUC), or whether it is an ad hoc group, with a special, once-and-for-all interest which is capable, at least theoretically, of complete satisfaction by political action; the Anti Corn Law League, CND, the groups favouring the abolition of capital punishment or the ending of apartheid in South Africa would all be examples. In each of these cases a policy could be enacted which would end the raison d'être of these latter groups – the ending of tariffs on imported corn (as occurred in 1846), the abolition of British nuclear weapons, repeal of all laws allowing for a death penalty or the ending by the South African Government of its policy of apartheid. Like CND, such groups may preserve an organization which can be turned to other causes, but if this happened, the aims of the organization would have changed, and thus it should be classified as a new group.

The second dimension concerns the purpose of the group – is it in essence a promotional group, which seeks to change the law or the policy of the government in some positive way, e.g. by promoting negotiations for entry into the Common Market, or the recognition of Rhodesian independence, or the ending of state aid to denominational schools, or votes at 18?, or is it primarily a defensive group, to oppose changes in policy which might affect the interests of group members – trade unions, or retailers, or coach operators threatened by nationalization, advertisers faced with the possibility of limitations on the use of media, villagers whose homes and amenities are endangered by the line of a new motorway? Without implying any rule of regularity, there is a tendency for ad hoc groups to be promotional, and permanent groups to be defensive (though with promotional aims from time to time), and for groups concerned with economic interests to be defensive (since most economic interests thrive best in a 'conservative' atmosphere) and groups concerned with social interests to be 'promotional' (i.e. 'radical'). Certainly this does not correspond to the left-wing – right-wing scale; indeed, the radical promotional groups can be found at both ends of such a scale, the defensive conservative groups in the centre. Goldwater's radical-right, fascism of the German, Italian, British or French types, right-wing nationalism of the kind associated with the German NPD or the Greek military junta are, in their own style, all as likely to be promotional as groups on the extreme left. This, too, on an international scale, is a feature of the Sino–Soviet ideological quarrels over Communism. The Chinese wish for 'permanent revolution', the Russians for the preservation of the status quo as being most conducive to their national political development.

Thirdly, there is the dimension of benefit – is the group concerned with the personal interests of its members, or with some external, and often generally beneficient cause? Again, there is an association between this dimension and that of the permanence of groups, but not a great deal. Both the AA and the RSPCA are permanent organizations, but the first is concerned with the interests of its motorist members, the second with animals, irrespective of whether they belong to members or not. The Campaign for Nuclear Disarmament and the Stansted lobby against the siting of the new airport were both ad hoc organizations – yet the first was primarily concerned with the dangers of nuclear war as it would affect everyone in Britain, whether sympathizers with the campaign or not, the second with the grave and immediate effects on their own way of life of the decision where to site the airport, whatever the consequential injuries or benefits to people in Birmingham, Bootle or Bognor Regis.

Bearing these dimensions in mind, we can now turn to an over-view of some of the major groups in contemporary British politics, whether concerned with economic, social, cultural or 'political' policies.

The increased emphasis of government on economic matters has meant that, in consequence, groups concerned with *economic interests* have taken on greater political importance. There are three distinct levels of concern which can be distinguished, and, depending on the questions under consideration, one may find a mixture of various types of group involved in the problem. The first level is that of ownership/non-ownership – i.e. the trade unions, the employers' associations, the TUC and the Confederation of British Industry. The Miners' Union, the three railway unions, the Transport and General Workers' Union, the Seamen, the Engineers, the Electricians, the Draughtsmen's and Allied Technicians' Association and many others have all played important roles in trying to influence government policy on various matters, many of them through their representatives sitting as Members of Parliament. The parallel employers' federations have their own political concerns, but in terms of the second level of our classification, that of the type of employment, employees and employers may be found on the same side, requesting government protection from foreign competition, or special subsidies, or some legislative provision favourable to mining (e.g. over exploitation of North Sea fuels), or railways (the 1968 Transport Act), or agriculture (pricing and marketing policies), etc. Thirdly, there is a regional level of concern, and here one may find the employers and workers in a number of industries lobbying together in favour of special treatment on a regional basis – highland development in Scotland, fiscal relief for depressed areas, opposition to the closure of railways, pressure for the extension of a motorway, for the building of a new road-bridge, for the opening of a new deep-water port.

To these industrial groups must be added certain other interests which may possess only a nominal degree of organization, if any at all, yet may be powerful on account of, say, personal connections, traditional status of the occupation in society, or economic importance. Consumers, the military, the Civil Service, the financial interests of the City of London, and many of the professions would be included in this sub-category, in so far as their political influence is not to be measured by paper-membership of an organization, by the size of a political fund or the number of sponsored MPs they can claim.

Social-cultural groups are those whose basis of connection is not primarily economic (though, since economics underlies most social questions to some degree, the economic aspects of policy will rarely be irrelevant), but rather some social characteristic or interest. It is less easy to classify such groups than was the case with economic groups, but it is possible to point to various salient aspects of modern society and identify some of the groups and interests which belong to them.

Among the oldest of these are the churches, and the influence of the established churches of England and Scotland, the nonconformist and Roman Catholic denominations, the Jews, and many other denominational or inter-denominational groups can be found to be indicated by examples ranging from the seventeenth-century constitutional questions such as the Civil War and the Whig Settlement, to the anti-slavery agitation of the eighteenth and nineteenth centuries, the problems of Ireland in the twentieth century, and now the reforms of the present period concerned with divorce law, capital punishment, the treatment of coloured immigrants and the delicate questions of abortion legislation and family planning. Civil questions concerning security, law and order, punishment and the liberties of the subject have often attracted the attention of interests and groups. Organizations concerned with problems of racial discrimination, such as CARD (Campaign Against Racial Discrimination), are examples in this category, along with the all-party group of lawyers called 'Justice', the National Council for Civil Liberties, the Howard League for Penal Reform, the professional bodies of barristers and solicitors, and the lobbies that have sprung up from time to time to campaign for specific changes in the legal code.[4]

As education has come to be more and more affected, and even controlled, by the government rather than by private organizations during the past sixty years, so correspondingly greater problems have arisen which groups and interests have sought to influence. While it may be said not unfairly that the professional bodies of the education world (e.g. the National Union of Teachers, the Association of Teachers in Technical Institutions, the Association of University Teachers, and so on) have been at least as much concerned with the economic problems of education as with its organization and direction, nonetheless these groups have played important roles in influencing policy on such diverse matters as the school-leaving age, comprehensive education, the place of the independent sector, and the expansion of higher education. This has been done by giving evidence to the various committees which have been set up to consider specific problems (and education has been the policy-area which has concerned perhaps the most such committees in the past twenty-five years), by representations to the government and to various Members of Parliament, through spokesmen in the Commons itself, and through local action by influence on public opinion in forums, parent-teacher bodies, intervention in election campaigns, protests to

[4] See, for example, the work by J.B. Christoph, *Capital Punishment and British Politics* (Allen and Unwin, 1962).

local authority education committees, etc. Though parent-teacher associations are neither as numerous nor as politically-influential in Britain as in the United States, still the parents of schoolchildren can be politically mobilized in matters of local importance (e.g. the Bristol grammar-school lobby in 1964), and to some extent nationally through petitions, letters to politicians and their votes. Two other organizations must be mentioned also, each with interests in different sectors of education – the Headmasters' Conference of the more famous public schools, and the National Union of Students. More recently, there has arisen a rather formless, but active, student interest also.

Transport and communications are essential functions in modern societies. So it is not surprising that they have generated powerful groups concerned with influencing the policies that may affect them. The Automobile Association and the Royal Automobile Club are concerned with the interests of motorists. The National Council on Inland Transport has played an important and not ineffective part in opposing indiscriminate railway closures. Even the ramblers' and cyclists' groups have been brought into politics on occasion by the consideration of policies affecting the countryside, the provision of footpaths and cycle tracks, etc. In broadcasting, the history of the commercial television lobby has already been the subject of a case-study;[5] the seemingly unsuccessful commercial radio lobby has not yet found its scholar, though no doubt there is a similar story to be told there. Mrs Mary Whitehouse has organized a group to bring pressure to bear on the authorities to 'clean up' aspects of broadcasting which offend the sensitive tastes of a section of the audience of listeners and viewers. In the press world, the Newspaper Proprietors' Association is a powerful influence, as are the organizations concerned with advertising, and the National Union of Journalists. The Press Council, being a semi-official body, cannot properly be classed as an organization seeking to influence government policy.

Such a cataloguing of groups and interests with social concerns could be continued at much greater length, but this brief

[5] H. Wilson, *Pressure Group: the Campaign for Commercial Television* (Secker & Warburg, 1961).

study must conclude with some reference to the causes which are one of the more generous and noble aspects of the British political scene. The importance of the movers and shakers associated with these causes, as examples of purposeful selflessness, and also as illustrations of successful influence on slothful, obdurate or incompetent government bodies, is indicated both by the familiarity of many of their names to young people, and by the statues, memorials, biographies, charities and public buildings that commemorate their fame. William Wilberforce, Elizabeth Fry, Florence Nightingale, Edwin Chadwick, Octavia Hill, Annie Besant, and more recently names such as Alan Herbert and Sydney Silverman, all have taken up some cause which needed attention, and, with a degree of commitment which in itself has been an important political weapon, have organized, lobbied, challenged, persuaded and debated on behalf of that cause – be it the slave, the prisoner, the Crimean wounded, the public health or the housing of the nineteenth-century slum population, the rights of women, the inequities of an anomalous divorce law, or the degrading institution of capital punishment. Other causes have been served by the unnamed, yet persevering, officials of the many organizations such as the National Society for the Prevention of Cruelty to Children, the League against Cruel Sports, or the many groups concerned with mental health, physical recreation, marriage guidance, or the welfare of old people. Though no government can be expected to try to satisfy all such groups immediately and without consideration, nonetheless there is now a readiness to listen which is in itself an enormous improvement on nineteenth-century practice.

Finally, there are groups with avowedly *'political'* aims to press forward, though these are few, due to the width of interests accommodated in the major parties. As with economics, of course, politics underlies all group action, in the sense that influence on policy is by its nature political, but when a group is categorized as 'political' in the sense used here, it means that its purpose is to alter some aspect of the institutions or processes of the political system itself. One difficulty is to distinguish such groups from parties, and many are in fact associated with the parties: the Scottish, Welsh and Irish 'home rule' groups are examples. But some instances of interests and groups in recent history which have not been 'quasi-parties' have occurred: the suffragette movement, Chartism, the republican groups of the 1870s, the Electoral Reform Society, and, in a more specific yet ephemeral sense, the ad hoc groups associated with the reform of local government in the London area in the early 1960s.

THE METHODS OF GROUP ACTION

How do these various groups seek to influence policy? Why does one group co-operate with a government department on a friendly basis, while another organizes sit-down demonstrations in Whitehall? What is the relationship between groups and political parties? Why do groups attempt to persuade individual MPs to support their cause when they must appreciate that party discipline will generally outweigh even the most telling of arguments? Do groups in fact 'run the country' or are they only the props used for the real drama of party conflict played on the political stage?

Before looking at these questions and their answers, a word of exposition. It is important not to attribute superhuman powers to groups, nor to see politics as a kind of conspiracy in which every mistake, every false move or broken promise is later rationalized as part of a Machiavellian scheme. Politicians, even 'group' politicians, err, make blunders, misinterpret situations, act hastily on the basis of subjective rather than objective factors. So it is necessary to remember that what the leadership of a group may perceive as being the best strategy by which to influence the government or Parliament may, to an external observer, appear to be inappropriate or foolish. What is to be emphasized is that leaders of groups act on the basis of a 'target structure', i.e. an appreciation of the most suitable parts of the political system on which to exert influence or 'pressure'.

Since Britain is not a federal state, in the way in which the USA or West Germany are, the points of access to the decision-makers are correspondingly fewer, and, if one leaves aside local government institutions and particular cases such as the Northern Ireland Cabinet and Parliament, are restricted basically to public opinion (by which is meant primarily the electorate), the parties, MPs and parliamentary candidates, Parliament, and the administration (the cabinet and the departments).

Most groups will take *public opinion* into account when considering a strategy of persuasion, if only because a negative reaction from the public can influence the views of MPs and officials, at least to the extent of providing them with an excuse to oppose the wishes of a group to which they were unsympathetic anyway. An additional dimension to such considerations has been added by the expansion and greater sophistication of opinion polling. But few groups will rely on the persuasion of the general public or the electorate being sufficient to change government action in any decisive fashion. The weight of persuasion required to swing, say, even 1 per cent of the electorate on a national basis from opinion A to opinion B *to an extent sufficient to alter their vote at an election* is beyond the means of all but the wealthiest groups. Public opinion is important because it can provide a climate of possibility. In other words, while public opinion may not in itself favour a particular change, it can permit the case for a change to be debated, and if necessary it will then accept such a change, even if the opinion-polls show a majority as still apathetic or opposed to the change. The abolition of capital punishment, the application to join the Common Market, re-nationalization of the steel industry and statutory control of income increases are all illustrations of this, and it can be supposed that the end of public executions, votes for women, and the introduction of compulsory education would also have been opposed by a majority of the electorate of the day.

But some groups will, *faute de mieux*, have to look to public opinion for support and for influence if they are to have any success at all. Many 'political' groups (of the kind discussed above) are of this type, if only because their aims are not likely to commend themselves to the existing occupiers of the seats of political power. But a more recent and obvious case of this is the Campaign for Nuclear Disarmament.

This movement, composed of a number of groups, interests and individuals, lacked any firm organizational basis. Thus it was not able to develop a politically experienced bureaucracy to deal with strategy, to direct the exertion of influence at parliamentary or party levels (though the Labour Party was persuaded to accept favourable motions at its 1960 Scarborough Conference), or to deal with government departments on a co-operative basis. Under a Conservative government, sensitive to challenges to its defence policy, CND had little hope of persuading the party leadership in the Cabinet to change its views, nor did it possess any technical expertise of the sort the departments might have found useful. A circular effect built up: lack of success at other levels diverted the efforts of the campaign towards publicity and public opinion. This in turn made the movement seem more objectionable to all but a handful of Members of Parliament, and when civil disobedience became the strategy of the 'Committee of One Hundred' – a challenge to the authority of the government which, like the General Strike, it could not ignore – the public became the only possible target which remained available, following the reversal in 1961 of the resolutions of Scarborough by the Labour Party, and the refusal of the Liberal Party to accept unilateral policies as its platform. Despite temporary upsurges in the opinion polls, despite its radical appeal to young people (especially students, to whom its badge became the symbol of conformity within the student community) publicity and public interest in the movement both died down, and the accession of a Labour Government in 1964 did nothing to improve the situation for CND. The question never became a live electoral issue, nor did the independent CND candidate at Twickenham in the 1964 election make any impact.

While not underestimating the possibilities of influencing public opinion – the Smethwick defeat of Patrick Gordon-Walker can be attributed partly to group efforts to persuade the public of the dangers of continued immigration – it is perhaps the least rewarding of the possible targets available, though in many cases it must be included in a 'strategy-mix' where radical changes of policy are desired.

The parties are an important target, as has already been suggested in earlier chapters. Decision-making within the formal institutions of the party can be important, if not crucial, to the policies eventually executed by the parties when in office. There are three important aspects of the party-group relationship:

(i) Many groups have close traditional, empirical and even administrative links with parties, which will give them added leverage when policies relevant to their group interests are being considered. The reverse side of the coin is that this close association may militate against exercise of influence on the other party when it is in power. For the Labour Party, the affiliated trade-unions, the Trades Union Congress, and the Co-operative movement (especially via the Co-operative Party) are obviously linked closely through similarity of ideological aims, through administrative and financial ties and through overlapping leadership. To a lesser *formal* extent, the free professions such as law and medicine, financial and commercial groups, the Confederation of British Industry and the National Farmers' Union may be considered as generally Conservative in sympathy. It is one of the weaknesses of the Liberal Party that no such list can now be drawn up of groups associated with that party. A consequence of such links is that a Conservative government will not find much electoral advantage in placating the unions, except in so far as labour unrest is blamed on the Government by Conservative or 'floating' voters, nor will a Labour government feel over-sympathetic to the demands of, say, investors or directors, with the proviso again that the economic situation may counsel some concessions to these groups.

(ii) Many party members at all levels of the party will also be members of groups, or will be sympathetic towards interests of various kinds. While generally party loyalty and party discipline will prevail in any conflict of interest for an MP, or a party official, if not for the rank-and-file party members, nevertheless such group interests will not be without influence. This influence may be exercised in debate, in polemics in party organs, in voting within party meetings, and by lobbying in the party. Nuclear disarmament, the Rhodesian situation, immigration control, incomes policy and comprehensive education are recent examples of policies which have exercised the leaders of one or more of the major parties, and over which it can be confidently assumed that various group-sponsored or 'interested' Members will have had a major voice in discussion.

(iii) The parties recognize the importance of groups and interests within the electorate, and make direct appeals to them. This may be found particularly during election campaigns, when speeches (like the famous Chatham speech of Mr Wilson in 1964: 'Why do I emphasize the importance of the Royal Navy?' Heckler: 'Because you're in Chatham!'), specific policy pamphlets, manifestoes, and photographs of leading politicians side by side with group representatives or in situations likely to appeal to certain interests (on farms, visiting hospitals or inspecting schools) are commonplace. Nor is this all entirely due to a desire to win votes. Party leaders are sagacious enough to appreciate that, while they have much to offer to groups, equally they can benefit from group advice, consultation and expertise when it comes to framing specific policies, whether on the decimalization of the currency, new regulations for foot-and-mouth disease, or the law regarding the privileges and responsibilities of trade unions.

Members of Parliament and candidates. The first occasion on which a candidate will realize the readiness of groups to intercede with legislators – whether actual or prospective – is at an election. The mail will contain dozens of circulars, open letters, appeals and brochures concerning the merits of particular policies, and some will request the favour of a reply to one or more questions, which will be carefully preserved against the day when a Bill comes forward affecting the interests of the group. Such a record serves two purposes: it identifies among the elected Members those who signified favourable (or unfavourable) attitudes, and it enables the group to invoke such replies in persuasion of a Member's vote in any division that may occur. Two defences are open to candidates – to ignore such importuning, or to plead party loyalty as a reason for not endorsing their given opinion by a vote in a division.

For tactical reasons groups may publish the answers (or the failure to answer) of candidates during an election campaign. This then may, it is supposed, influence members of the group or sympathizers who will vote for the candidate most favourably disposed to the group's interests, or at least will avoid voting for hostile candidates. Similarly parsons have been known to suggest to their congregations which of the candidates are inclined to favour Sunday observance, and the author, as a parliamentary candidate, was invited to face questions from various group representatives during the 1964 campaign, including members of the local branches of the National Union of Teachers and the National Farmers' Union. Once elected, the Member's daily routine will begin with the mail, which will generally contain several messages pertaining to group policies; the day may continue with meetings with lobbyists, or sponsored Members anxious to press a case, or listening to speeches delivered in the House by spokesmen for this union, or that industry, or the other charitable foundation, cause, movement or what have you. The day may well conclude with attendance at a supper given by the Anglo–German Parliamentary Group, or by being an honoured guest at a fund-raising meeting for the promotion of some campaign aimed at procuring a change in the policy of the government.

Parliament, so obviously a target which can reward the skilful application of pressure by passing favourable legislation or at least by accepting suitable amendments to otherwise unfavourable Bills, is, in some ways, hardly a target at all. Parliament itself is, after all, composed of its Members, and we have already discussed the ways in which groups may attempt to influence MPs, either as party supporters or as individual representatives. Yet it must be allowed that there is an additional element to a campaign which seeks to affect the decisions of Parliament over and above that of pressure on the MP. This extra dimension is the extent to which the group already has sympathizers, or, better, spokesmen, within the Commons or the Lords, and thus the group can make out its case more freely, less inhibited by the natural wariness of the MP towards 'external' persuasion.

These affiliations of MPs are either publicized (in *Dod's Parliamentary Companion* or *The Times' Book of the House of Commons*), or can be checked quite openly. In any case, there is the convention of disclosure which must be complied with whenever an interested Member makes an intervention.

Various procedural devices are available by which spokesmen for groups may intervene in the parliamentary process. Question-time can be utilized for eliciting information (though generally groups will be able to obtain more readily the same information – though with less publicity – by direct approaches to departments); it is also an opportunity to reveal the embarrassment of a Minister over sensitive matters of policy, and this can be employed as a useful political tactic, for instance when a Minister is obviously loth to commit himself to a particular course of action.

Contributions to debate from group spokesmen are frequent. It may be that a Member wishes to put, quite openly, the case for a particular interest; possibly he may wish to use his known contact with a group to establish his extra authority to speak about the matter under debate; or he may even initiate debate by use of an adjournment motion or similar device, in order to further the aims of a group or interest. The debate may even be the result of a Private Members' ballot, which gives a small number of Members the opportunity to put forward a Bill or motion to be debated in the House. Among such debates in recent years which have clearly been concerned with particular interests or groups (though not necessarily in any way sponsored by them) have been: 28 January 1966 (Estate agents); 18 February 1966 (Mentally handicapped children); 3 February 1967 (Public service and armed forces pensioners); 10 February 1967 (Small-business owners); 16 February 1968 (Persons excluded from National Insurance pensions schemes); 1 March 1968 (Caravan dwellers); 15 March 1968 (Disabled and the chronic sick).

All the devices associated with the parliamentary party are also available. Matters can be raised at party meetings, whether of the full parliamentary party or the various subject-committees, such as Defence or Home Affairs. Efforts can be directed towards the setting-up of a new committee – on a permanent or an ad hoc basis – to deal with a particular topic, which would give it more party attention and significance than if it was dealt with by a more general committee. Lobbying for a particular cause can be undertaken on a party basis, or party MPs can be asked to join an all-party committee, if this is thought to be the appropriate body to press some matter forward. The story of the commercial television lobby, in H. Wilson's *Pressure Group*, illustrates many of these devices in use, and is a classic study of a successful parliamentary effort by a lobby.

It is not surprising, though, that in an age when the general description of British government is in terms of 'Cabinet government' or 'rule by civil servants' or 'the decline of

Parliament', pressure from groups should concentrate on influencing the *administrative machine*. The spectacular campaign aimed at public opinion, the occasional success of group action in Parliament – these attract the attention of the press, and, rather too often, the scholars of political science. Yet the majority of group successes, and the greater part of the efforts of groups, are associated with the exercise of influence on the Executive.

There are many reasons for this. First, there is the problem of party discipline in Parliament. An organized lobby in 1869 could still hope to influence a number of Members sufficiently for them to disregard party and vote for a Bill or an amendment in the way the group desired. Little, if any, sanction from the party would be likely to follow. Today, a century later, a three-line whip is generally defied only at the risk of punishment ranging from a reprimand to expulsion from the party (which means, in effect, the loss of the nomination for a seat at the next general election, unless the miscreant is re-admitted to the party). So groups can only modify, rarely defeat, hostile legislation against the wishes of the government party. But when a Bill is passed into law, there is often considerable scope for its administration, and here party discipline is far less effective. Ministers, and their civil servants, can be persuaded to exercise their powers in the most favourable manner by various arguments as to equity, efficiency, co-operation, and so on, all without defeating the broad intention of Parliament. A second reason is simply the increasing technical complexity of administration. Groups are often the chief sources of technical information, of co-operation in executing policies, of constructive criticism of draft legislation, and so forth, and, in return, they can hope to influence matters in ways favourable to their interests. This is not necessarily improper or unethical; it is not necessarily against the public interest, especially if the group's case is argued openly and fairly. Certainly there is a close correspondence between private and public interests in the minds of, say, doctors favouring changes in the administration of the National Health Service, teachers lobbying for a higher school-leaving age or increased facilities for teacher-training, farmers negotiating a higher subsidy for rearing beef cattle, or the Automobile

Association pressing for an increase in the rate of motorway construction. Thirdly, new legislation does not spring out of thin air; most of it emanates from Ministers and their departments. Some of this legislation will probably be favourably received by Parliament once it is brought before them; other Bills will arouse little or no hostility or favour simply because they appear unimportant, except to affected interests. Thus influence with departments may be directed towards affecting the priorities of administrators, rather than just persuading them of the merits of a Bill. Action, rather than simply agreement, is the target.

One other reason for the importance of the administrative sector in the plans of groups is the homogeneity of the leadership and executive personnel of both the public office and the group headquarters. Basically, this relies on common educational and social experiences: the Under-Secretary at the Ministry and the Executive Secretary of the group may well have attended the same (or a similar) school, the same Oxbridge University and be members of the same London club. With a Labour Government, the differences in social background of party leaders compared to the Conservatives can still mean there are contacts like these, if with different groups. An illustration is the experience of Frank Cousins, a Minister in the Wilson Government who later returned to his former post as General Secretary of one of Britain's most powerful trade unions, the Transport and General Workers'. Yet there is a further factor of similarity, which is at least as important as accidents of schooling or family background – the shared profession of political administration. There will be a common respect, a common sympathy between administrators from the public and private sectors that will be different from their attitudes towards the general group membership or elected representatives such as MPs, just as there is mutual sympathy among MPs of all parties which does not include civil servants.

This implies three things concerning group relations with ministries and boards. First, communication will be improved between them by all sorts of informal contacts and unofficial links. Lunch at 'the Club', the phone call from a group official to his acquaintance in the Ministry of X, a conversation over sherry at a professional convention on the topic with which they're both concerned – these are advantages that new, or 'hostile', groups will not receive in their dealings with government, because mutual trust and respect will not have developed. Second, co-operation, because each side knows it will be able to rely on a quid pro quo – again, it must be emphasized, no impropriety is implied – when the need arises. The department may want to show certain factories to a group of foreign representatives; contact with the relevant trade association produces an interesting and hospitable schedule in days, rather than weeks, or longer, if it had been necessary to arrange it through official channels. In return, a request from the association for certain statistics may be dealt with immediately rather than in three months' time if processed according to routine. Thirdly, there is the common interest of both sides in legislation and the administration of policy: that it should be as efficient, and as fair, as possible, having regard for the public interest. This is more likely to be the case when the officials and the group representatives are concerned with the achievement of these ends, rather than the attainment (or the prevention) of political advantage. Thus the contacts between the two sides aids this process, by allowing both sides to take positions or make concessions which they would not be prepared to do if they feared publicity of negotiation. This has its dangers, but on balance probably the political process benefits.

THE ORGANIZATION OF GROUPS

The organizational structure of groups varies widely. Some, such as trade unions or industrial organisations, have a democratic representational basis by which groups elect local leaders, who in turn elect area and national executives. Others, mainly groups concerned with benefits external to their sympathizers or members (such as CND or various charitable causes) pay less regard to representation, and often rely on volunteer leaders who find it easy to keep their posts, if only because there is little competition to assume the burdens of unpaid office. In such organizations, democratic representation is a value low on the scale of group priorities; achievement and moral attitudes are considered of greater importance.

In all groups, political skills will be important. Communications, the ability to obtain funds, publicity and membership, the arts of conciliation and persuasion, plus, above all, appropriate leadership (for some groups charismatic, personalized, publicity-conscious leaders, for example, for others those who are conciliatory, administratively-talented, unassuming) – these will be valued, and will be of value, in considering how successfully a group achieves its stated purposes.

THE BALANCE OF GROUPS

Those who, as democrats, criticize the political role of interests and pressure-groups, do so usually on the grounds that they press for benefits of a 'partial' nature, and that in doing so they endanger the possibility of the government and Parliament attending to the public interest or (for those mindful of Rousseau) the 'general will' of society. It is therefore of importance that so many interests and groups tend to balance each other, or at least compete for the attention of politicians, their time, and the public resources they can allocate. There is a kind of 'countervailing power' in the exercise of political, as well as economic, influence.[6] Thus, in Britain, the Trades Union Congress has a natural opposite in the Confederation of British Industry, and the individual unions in the equivalent employers' associations. In the field of transport, groups try to protect the interests of their particular concern – the Road Haulage Association, the coastal shippers, canal users, the motorists organizations, the bus companies, the transport unions, etc. 'Causes' have also produced groups on both sides; while no group advocates cruelty to animals or children, groups are or were in existence to press for Britain's entry into the Common Market, and to press for Britain's continued self-exclusion; to keep Sunday as a day of worship and little else, and to obtain the relaxation of the ancient statutory prohibitions on Sunday entertainment and leisure; to obtain a commercial television channel, and to oppose one; to ban hunting and similar sports, and to promote them; to encourage unilateral disarmament by Britain, and to discourage such

[6] The concept is discussed in J.K.Galbraith, *American Capitalism: The Concept of Countervailing Power* (Penguin, 1963), pp. 125 ff.

renouncement of nuclear weapons pending multilateral disarmament.

In this way, groups serve to highlight particular issues and to promote debate on them. In such cases, both sides of the problem will be presented, and facts, arguments, illustrations will be marshalled in support of each case. Aided by the developments of the mass media, the greater public interest in political issues, and the wider latitude given to government as a function in society, pressure-groups may thus be regarded as an educative force, as well as being politically beneficial.

But – the critics have a point when they argue that there is no guarantee that *both* sides of a case will be presented, or that there *are* only two sides to any question of public importance. Until recently, one of the greatest interests in the country lacked cohesion or organization, and its membership was practically unprotected – the consumer. Even today the interests of pensioners, young people, widows, the industrially-disabled, and the rate-payer are hardly represented (at least nationally) other than by individual Members of Parliament or through officials of various social services.

And, though it may be rather an unfashionable view, it is still possible to make out a case for recognizing the existence of a 'public interest' apart from the interests of competing parties over an issue. It is in the public interest that a labour dispute does not disrupt services or supplies to the consumer, that union demands and employers' concessions do not lead to inflation, that political argument in Britain over immigration or Rhodesian independence or the Viet-Nam war does not escalate into public disorder. Members of Parliament, ministers, civil servants, and local government officials and councillors are all charged with a responsibility towards the welfare of society as a whole. This may be met by attention to the demands of groups and interests, but there will be occasions when a wider view will be required, and this obligation should not then be overlooked.

So it is to the question of the relation between the general values of society and the more specific values of groups and political parties that the next chapter looks.

6 Groups and policy

Parties and pressure-groups exist for particular purposes, and these purposes have much to do with the word 'policy'. So far, this book has focused mainly on what goes to make up political parties and other political groups, how they developed into their contemporary form, and how they are organized and led. This is by no means the whole story.

Policy is itself only one stage in the 'ladder of values' which is discussed later in this chapter. It is derived from the basic values (or what will henceforth be termed the 'ideology') of parties and groups, and itself gives rise to more specific proposals, which may be termed a 'programme' or a series of 'decisions', which are intended to implement policies. So we arrive at a relationship which is one of the ways of defining the activity of politics itself. Groups are concerned with influencing policy; policy is the subject-matter of politics; politics is the activity by which decisions are made in an authoritative fashion which affect society – generally by the allocation of resources among several competing claims for priorities. This view of politics has been succinctly expressed as: 'Who gets what, when and how?'[1]

Of course, not all the transactions that go to make up day-to-day social life are 'political'. A packet of frozen peas, a pint of beer, an allocation of time and space at a parking meter, the services of a window-cleaner, a seat at a theatre – these are allocated through the price mechanism within the economic system. The morning service at the parish church, the help of a neighbour with the construction of a garden shed, the voluntary efforts of prison visitors or the local hospital 'League of Friends' – these are allocated through social mechanisms. The distinctive features of *political* allocation are: first, that it is an authoritative process, and is supported by the sanctions of the legal and coercive institutions of the state (fines, imprisonment, injunctions, confiscations of goods, etc.), and second, that such

[1] H.Lasswell's title of his book on politics: *Politics, Who Gets What, When, How* (Meridian Books, USA, 1958).

decisions are basically of concern to the whole of society generally, even though the subject-matter may appear particular or partial. For example, increased penalties for drunken driving apparently do not concern pedestrians directly, yet the law applies to them if and when they become drivers. In contrast, the purchase of an item in a shop, or a decision not to purchase because the price is too high, is an individual decision, of no concern other than to the parties to the bargain. Similarly, a voluntary social action (provided that it does not break the law of the land) is again only of concern to the participants, e.g. a decision to aid a sick neighbour, or to undertake voluntary work for some charity. On the other hand, recent legislation has made political certain forms of discriminatory social behaviour on grounds of race that previously were only social.

What has all this to do with groups? Simply this, that political parties exist, as has already been pointed out, to gain office in order to control the priorities of such political allocation − more guns, less butter; more help for needy families, less troops East of Suez; taxes imposed on capital gains, higher rates of unemployment pay; more attention to higher education in the technical colleges, less to the Universities; more effort to reduce road deaths, less to close unremunerative railway lines; high priority to the reform of local government and the Civil Service, low priority to the reform of the House of Lords or the public schools; trade unions reform along with an incomes policy. Pressure-groups, lobbies and interests exist to influence the direction or the priority given to some decision, or some policy-area, in particular − nuclear disarmament, equal pay for women, Sunday Observance, government aid to farming, or the ending of discriminatory practices on the grounds of race.

THE 'LADDER OF VALUES'

It has been suggested that political decisions result from policies, and that policies are attempts to deal with political problems by reference to a set of basic values, or an ideology. This does not mean that every decision of Parliament, every action of a Minister of Housing and Local Government, is first measured against some statement of principles such as the party constitution, or the more abstract of Disraeli's speeches. Nor does it imply any historical sequence. The Conservative and Liberal parties, in particular, were built up on the basis of personal attitudes towards a series of immediate questions, from which groups emerged who recognized that they favoured similar policies, and these similarities grew, as it were, into a set of values. But the concept of a 'ladder of values' is useful in political analysis, for it allows an observer better to comprehend otherwise seemingly meaningless disputes such as the Labour Party's quarrel over Clause IV and revisionism, the Asquith–Lloyd George divisions in the Liberal Party (or the later Samuelite–Simonite split in the Party in the 1930s), and the travails of the rejected Conservative Party in the 1945–51 period.

It also permits a more understanding attitude towards day-to-day disputes within contemporary parties. Many of these are, on the face of it, quarrels over the merits of policies in certain fields, e.g. the decision to withhold the right of entry to Kenyans with British passports, the implementation of the incomes freeze, attitudes towards negotiations with the Rhodesian regime, immigration policy. Yet in many of these cases, the several disputants may claim to favour the same ends, though each would defend his method as the more likely to achieve them; or, if forced to concede a difference on the merits of policy in general, dissension from the party line would be in the name of the preservation of the basic principles of the party.

The consequences of such disputes for the leadership must not be overlooked. Because basic values are so frequently expressed in vague or ambiguous language ('democracy', 'freedom', 'the dictatorship of the proletariat', 'putting Britain first') a need arises for an adjudicator who can interpret these generalities authoritatively in terms of current policies and programmes. This role falls to the Leader of the Party, though if it seems that his interpretation is too novel or too radical he may be challenged by sections of the party. Gladstone, Disraeli, Lloyd George, MacDonald and Hugh Gaitskell were all faced with opposition to their interpretations of party ideology at various periods of their leadership. The Conservative Party seems more ready than the Labour Party to permit its Leader to exercise such powers of interpretation, since Conference and the National Executive modify the freedom of the Labour Leader to a considerable extent.

To illustrate the relationship between ideology, policy and programme, first we return to the 1966 manifestoes, where all three elements are to be found; after this, two examples of parliamentary legislation – one from the Conservative Administration of 1951–64, and one from the present Labour Administration – will serve as brief case studies to give an indication of how the 'ladder of values' operates in practice.

The basic statement of Labour's ideology is its Constitution, which all members of the Party must agree to accept. The latest application of this ideology can be found in the Party's 1966 election manifesto, in such terms as these:

> the motive and inspiration of Labour remain, and always will remain, to secure the prosperity and welfare of all the people . . .
> . . . We have started on the long process of modernizing obsolete procedures and institutions, ending the dominance of vested interests, liberating the forces of youth and building a New Britain.
> At its simplest, our aim is to extend to the whole community what the responsible citizen wishes for himself and his family.

Midway between ideology and general policy come such typical manifesto-promises as these four 'central objectives of its policy'; the maintenance and improvement of the social services; the establishment of priorities in public spending which would protect housing, schools, hospitals and the regions of highest unemployment; the maintenance of full employment and a high level of industrial investment; the longer term reconstruction of Britain through a National Plan. More specific statements of policy were also made, such as:

> We shall further develop co-operation between nationalized industries to cut out waste; we shall set out more precise targets to guide their investment and price policy in the national interest.
> We must move towards greater fairness in the rewards for work.
> . . . We shall introduce major reforms in local finance.
> . . . We shall greatly improve the collection, processing and organization of government information and statistical services.

The important point to note here is that such statements can be tested by asking later: 'Have you in fact achieved this policy?' even though such proposals can be implemented in several different ways.

In some cases, the manifesto includes quite precise details of the way in which such proposals are to be implemented. To give just one illustration, rents and mortgages: policies will be carried through by (a) a Leasehold Enfranchisement Bill, (b) financial relief to local authorities to keep down increases in council house rents, (c) a mortgage option scheme to assist buyers on mortgage who do not benefit from income tax relief. All three of these schemes have been put into practice, even though Parliament added some amendments to some aspects of them, whereas the more general policy statements only provided the basis for such specific decisions.

The basic values of the Conservative Party come mainly from its history, modified by pragmatism, and as interpreted – chiefly – by its Leader. This allows the Party more freedom at the level of policy, for it is difficult to challenge a policy proposal as being obviously out-of-line with ideology. The time element in any case allows the Leader to claim that what was inappropriate twenty years ago might be necessary to the Party under contemporary conditions. 'Conservatives are prepared to conserve the measures of their opponents, as well as their own.'[2] Thus Conservative Leaders have accepted many things about which their predecessors had grave doubts – the welfare state, the mixed economy, the desirability of membership of the European Economic Community, the principle of comprehensive secondary education.

It is not, therefore, very surprising to find in the manifesto of the Conservative Party – the programme of an opposition party, after all – a lack of ideological statement, and an abundance of policy and programme proposals, often contrasting the situation they intend to bring about with that which exists under Labour rule.

Its five primary policies are clearly stated: 'to get the economy straight', 'reform the trade unions', 'remodel the Welfare State', 'get the nation properly housed', 'restore respect for Britain'. These are statements to which the question 'how?' can justly be applied. The 'how?' is answered by the more precise programme statements which follow. They

[2] T.Raison, *Why Conservative?* (Penguin, 1964), p. 41.

include, in the section 'to improve industrial relations' for example:

> Pass a new Industrial Relations Act. . . .
> Ensure that agreements between unions and employers are kept by making them legally enforceable.
> Establish a registrar of trade unions and employers' associations.
> Set up a new industrial court. . . .
> Repeal the Trade Disputes Act 1965 so as to help prevent intimidation.

Each of these is specific enough as a proposal to be the subject of a new Act of Parliament, or a directive to a ministerial department if parliamentary powers already suffice.

These were all statements concerning the future. If one looks back to the past, to the five years of Labour's administration or the thirteen years of Conservative government which preceded them, there are plentiful examples of programmes which derived from policies, and which are clearly related to the basic values of each party.

One such proposal was the Resale Price Maintenance Act of July 1964, by which the Conservative Government severely restricted the possibilities of suppliers enforcing agreements on retailers relating to the price at which the goods were to reach the public. This Act originated in a private Member's Bill introduced by a Labour back-bencher, John Stonehouse, in 1963. His Bill was not pressed to a division on its Second Reading, because the Government had announced its own intention to legislate on the matter a few days earlier, stimulated, no doubt, by the indications of support that Stonehouse's Bill might obtain. Following the publication of a White Paper in March 1964, outlining the Government's proposals in the general field of restrictive practices, opposition from small shopkeepers, manufacturers, and various elements of the Party mounted. Despite this opposition, and after accepting a number of important amendments to the Bill, the Government prevailed, and the new measures became law.

The interest in this case lies in its degree of congruence with other Conservative policies, and with what were thought to be the basic values of the Party. This was, after all, the occasion for one of the most serious rebellions against the

Conservative leadership since it had gained power in 1951: eighteen Conservatives voted in favour of an amendment to kill the Bill, and at least a further twenty abstained.

The 'basic values' involved here were two-fold: the idea that society was best served by having as little government interference with business as possible (a logical position for an anti-Socialist party to take), and the related but distinctive idea that the alternative to a regulated economy was one in which restrictions of various kinds were removed, if necessary by government action. The opponents of the Bill stressed the first, the supporters the second of these two notions. Given that interference by the Government was necessary in order to permit greater competition in the economy, the policy of refusing to allow existing legal sanctions in support of monopolies and restrictive practices to continue could be seen as a proper way to achieve this, and the specific proposals concerning the abolition of resale price maintenance were in accord with this policy. As Mr Heath said of this Bill: 'It is one element, and an important element, in a comprehensive policy. The object of this policy is to promote more competition throughout the economy.' Whereas an opponent on the Conservative side, Sir Frank Markham, indicated that, for him at least, the issue went deeper than the Bill, or even the policy on which it was based:

> We are described as rebels because we are to adhere to policies which have been worked out in the past and have been re-affirmed consistently. We are not rebels. The rebels are on that Front Bench and in the Cabinet. It is they who have changed consistent Conservative policy adopted and approved over the years.[3]

A more recent example, this time concerning the Labour Government elected to office in 1964, was the legislation to return the steel industry to public ownership. The steel industry had been one of the last major targets of the nationalization programme of the post-war Labour Administration, and had been brought under state ownership after legislation to further curtail the delaying powers of the House of Lords had been passed, to prevent the Second Chamber from holding up nationalization for more than one year. The threats of the

[3] HC *Debates* (691), 10 March 1964, col. 255, 355–6.

Conservative opposition to undo this legislation were fulfilled when they returned to office in 1951. But the ideology of the Labour Party had remained unaltered in this respect, despite Gaitskell's unavailing attack on Clause IV (which referred to 'the common ownership of the means of production, distribution and exchange'). Both the basic philosophy of the Party and its desire for revenge on the Conservatives for undoing their earlier legislation on the subject impelled the Labour leadership to include the re-nationalization of steel in its 1964 manifesto.

Though this proposal did not in itself cause the division in the Party, it did symbolize the rift between the left-wingers who regarded the party constitution as the proper and correct source of policy for a Socialist Government, and wished to keep to the strict letter of Clause IV, and the revisionists who saw such fundamentalism as contributing to the poor image of the Party in the eyes of the electorate. They wanted the Labour Party to bring its ideology up-to-date, in line with, say, continental Socialist parties, such as the non-Marxist parties of West Germany and Scandinavia. They realized that any government which based its policies on the literal meaning of Clause IV would soon be in trouble, electorally (since polls showed that probably even a majority of Labour supporters were against any further nationalization), and economically. Unlike the Conservatives over Resale Price Maintenance, the Wilson Government could not go ahead with any legislation likely to divide the Party with only a single-figure majority to count on. Yet to ignore the question altogether would be to alienate many left-wing MPs, on whom Labour's majority also depended, and many party workers in the constituencies.

A White Paper was introduced in 1965, and, after a heated debate, with a dramatic last-minute offer by George Brown which won over the votes of two possible rebels (Woodrow Wyatt and Desmond Donnelly), the House accepted it as a basis for legislation by a majority of four votes. Twelve months later, now buttressed by a majority of 100, the Wilson Government introduced legislation on the basis of the White Paper, and the Bill became law on the 22 March 1967. However, no further attempts to nationalize industries directly have been made, though the consequences of other legislation, such as the Transport Bill (1968), may involve an increase in public ownership of economic assets that once were in private hands.

Again Hansard offers illustrations of what steel nationalization meant to some Labour MPs in terms of the Party's basic values. The Minister in charge of the White Paper, Mr Lee, saw it as part of the process of making British society more democratic, through state control of the 'commanding heights' of the economy:

> I do not believe that we look upon our democracy as something which rests merely on the universal franchise and the ballot box. Under our constitution, there can never have been in this country a Government with sufficient power to be able to offset the things which these great private monopolies may wish to do. I believe that if we are to progress with our democratic institutions, it is vitally important that these great power blocs should be brought within the confines of the national economy.

For Mr Wyatt, speaking for a revisionist view of Clause IV, the proposal for outright nationalization was a disappointment:

> I thought that we would, and we could, transform Clause Four into a new, living concept of how, in a democratic Government, control and ownership can be married with the legitimate private ambitions and enthusiasms of other people in industry. . . . This is exactly what the White Paper does not do for steel.

Later in the same speech he gave his view of the relationship between the policy proposed and the basic values of the Party:

> The country does not want this old-fashioned type of nationalization. The majority of Labour supporters do not want it to be given priority.

The other expected rebel, Mr Donnelly, put his position as follows:

> I myself have never been opposed to public ownership. I am in favour of public ownership where it serves the public interest. But it is not an end in itself. . . .[4]

In the debate on the Bill itself, the new Minister of Power, Mr Marsh, took a similar position, though he supported the Bill:

> I have never made a secret of the fact that I do not believe that

---

[4] The above quotations are all from HC *Debates* (711), 6 May 1965, cols. 1587–8, 1631, 1644 and 1668.

nationalization of itself necessarily solves anything. I think that frequently it is an essential means towards the achievement of desirable ends, but it can never be an end in itself. . . . I find the views of the very small band of those who believe in nationalization on principle somewhat illogical. . . .[5]

In neither debate did the extreme left-wing MPs attempt to put the ideological case for nationalization as a doctrine, though Michael Foot laid emphasis on the need to eliminate the power of the vested interests of privately owned steel companies. Yet, in a way, it was unnecessary to put such a case. The Bill secured the support of the leadership, and, with a majority of any substance, this guaranteed its passage. But steel nationalization was probably a pyrrhic victory for the Left. It was nationalized, but seemingly out of obeisance to the memory of the great days of the 1940s, rather than from a wholehearted belief in the nationalization of the 'means of production, distribution and exchange' as the ideological solution to problems of economic policy. In itself, the battle over steel was a sign that the basic values of the Party *had* been revised (could Mr Marsh have made his comment and remained in office if this were not so?) at least in effect, if not in form.

PARTIES AND VALUES

The two issues just examined show that, unlike American parties for instance, British political parties do regard their ideological foundations with gravity; yet, unlike some of the parties of the Right and of the Left which have haunted French, German, Spanish or Italian politics this century, they have not taken ideology so seriously as to endanger either their own identities or the ability of the parliamentary system to carry on the government of the country. The dialogue between the parties has always been modulated to reach the ear of the supporter, the voter, the citizen. Change has been painful and plentiful in the history of British parties: parliamentary reform for the Whigs, Corn Law repeal for the Tories, Irish home rule for Gladstone's Liberal Party, tariffs for Balfour's Conservatives, the welfare state for post-war Conservatives, a defence system based on nuclear weapons for the modern

[5] HC *Debates* (732), 25 July 1966, cols. 1228–9.

Labour Party. Yet the parties remain, absorbing the fissiparous effects of such controversies, so that a divided, thrice-defeated Labour Party could almost tear itself apart in 1960, yet brush aside the challenge of a reviving Liberal Party and form a government in 1964, and by 1966 gain a majority that it had taken the Conservatives eight years and three elections to attain. Meanwhile a defeated and dejected Conservative Party, under its third leader in four years, could recover within a year of its 1966 defeat to start a series of by-election victories and local government successes unmatched in the post-war period.

Why, then, do the parties manage to persist so successfully over time? And how do they adapt their basic ideologies so skilfully to take account of new moods, new needs, new situations in British politics?

For answers to these questions, it is best first to look once more to their histories. In the nineteenth century, the parties represented fairly general positions on the great questions of the day – industrialization, the future of agriculture, tariffs, social reform, fiscal policy, Ireland, and diplomatic problems. The political context forced the parties to be tolerant of deviations from the views of the leadership. In this way it was possible for Whigs and Radicals to belong to the Gladstonian Liberal Party, the Conservatives could survive the rebellions of the 'Fourth Party' and the social policies of Disraelian conservatism, and later it could absorb without too much upheaval the errant Liberals who followed Joseph Chamberlain across the floor after his resignation over Irish home rule in 1886. Yet certain issues did prove to be ideological barriers. (Here the contrast with the USA is clear, for it is difficult to find examples of parties being modified by ideological – as opposed to personal – differences. The 'Bull Moose' revolt of Theodore Roosevelt was primarily a matter of personality, and the same could be said of Wallace's Progressive Party in the 1948 election. Nor, as far as can be seen, did 1968 disprove this in either of the major parties.) Such issues included Irish home rule which lost Gladstone and the Liberals the support of the Unionists, and tariffs, where the Liberal Party lost some support to the Conservatives before the First World War, and again in the National Government in 1931, when Liberals who were prepared to abandon free trade became hybrid National Liberals, and from then onwards became almost indistinguishable, in effect, from Conservatives.

Also included as part of the political context are factors associated with government responsibility and the electoral and legislative framework. While allowing that for all three parties there are ultimate ideological boundaries which have to be accepted by supporters, these are wide in extent, not always well-defined, and within their limits there is much room for compromise Questions of political importance tend to become matters of for-or-against decisions taken by the government of the day. Amendment is not difficult to achieve, especially for purposes of improving the Bill, or securing a wider basis of agreement. Elections come to be regarded as verdicts on the performance of the Government rather than the selection of blocs of representatives of rigid ideological positions. One accepted, or rejected, the Conservative position of 1905, the continuation of the Lloyd George coalition in 1922, Labour's record in 1950 or 1951, the Conservative policies in 1959, or their management of social and economic problems in 1964. And because of this, the position of third parties is difficult to present within such a framework. In effect, the electoral system allows no provision for a vote of 'no, not this Government again – but not the Opposition either'.

So it comes to this: British government is fundamentally party government. Being the government forces the leadership of a party to match basic values with the possibilities of policy and the realities of the situation. Thus, while appearing not to change its ideological formation any more than a cliff on the coast appears to change its outline, in both cases erosion and modification take place. This operates on the Opposition also, to a lesser extent, because the need to appear responsible, coupled with the hope of office, limits the acceptability of rigid or extreme positions for their leadership as well. It is one of Harold Wilson's political talents that he realized this, and, by offering the more able of his left-wing colleagues responsibility as departmental ministers from 1964 onwards, he forced them to appreciate the need to apply values in a realistic, rather than in a doctrinal, fashion. And so the party of 'socialism' nationalizes no more industries for the present, finds itself unable unilaterally to abandon nuclear weapons, is forced to limit negotiated wage settlements within a predetermind 'norm', re-imposes prescription charges (at a higher rate than its opponents had imposed) despite its promises to maintain the principle of free prescriptions, and, in the names of efficiency and the export drive, encourages the concentration of industrial units in the private sector. The party of 'free enterprise' accepts the welfare state, along with the bulk of the nationalization programme, increases expenditure on the social services, and restrains the freedom of manufacturers to enforce resale prices. Circumstances change, and the parties change too – in programme, more slowly in policy, and slower still in ideology, but they change nevertheless.

This adaptability reduces the danger of party division, because the basic values of the Labour Party have been able in the past to include a Foot and a Donnelly, a Wyatt and a Crossman, a Crosland and a Barbara Castle. On the opposition benches a Powell and a Sandys can find sufficient agreement to remain in the same party as, say, a Boyle and a MacLeod. In the Liberal Party the variety of positions is as great – Bessell on the right, Wainwright and Steel on the left, representing the extremes in the parliamentary party. While the expulsion from time to time of Foot and Donnelly, or the dismissal of Enoch Powell from his shadow cabinet responsibilities, may promote rejoicing among the colleagues from whom they differ most, the reason for such disciplinary action *has* been discipline, not ideology. It is their refusal to submit to party rules or decisions that brings them trouble, not the views they have expressed. The result: no third party has started from the splintering of an existing parliamentary party this century.[6]

Even Aneurin Bevan, regarded by some as the major left-wing parliamentarian of the modern period, recognized these limitations of ideology in political practice: 'I have never regarded politics as the arena of morals. It is the arena of interests.'[7]

The importance of this fact is that so many influences can be said to affect day-to-day politics, so that utopian attempts

[6] Other than the 'one-man' new party which Donnelly has created (1969).
[7] Quoted in M.Foot, *Aneurin Bevan*, vol. I. (MacGibbon & Kee, 1962), p. 166.

to apply some set of unswerving principles, especially if they imply radical change, are doomed to failure. Even the Bolsheviks were forced to accept this in the first decade following their 1917 revolution in Russia, when the policies of radical socialism had to be modified or even postponed in the circumstances as they existed. There must be a schedule of priorities, which will cause some valued, but complicated or unfeasible, reforms to be laid aside. The multiple interests that Members of Parliament represent, or have represented to them by lobbies and pressure-groups, will affect their attitudes to legislation, and compromises will have to be sought. International influences will also limit what is possible for the government to carry out at any period of time, such as defence commitments, the balance of payments, tariff alterations, alliances, the procurement of imported raw materials and so on. Physical resources are limited, and other economic factors, e.g. a shortage of skilled manpower, will also have their effect. It may be fundamental policy to end the housing shortage – but where is the land to build on? Where are the builders and other craftsmen? Can the factories produce the bricks? Who is to pay the cost? And, most important question of all, what else is to be postponed in the meantime? It may be vital to put our balance of payments into surplus, but at what cost to the social services? at what cost in terms of interference with labour relations over wage limitations and unemployment? How can British governments affect the terms of trade, or EEC competition, or revaluation of other currencies, or preemption of our export markets by Swiss or German or Japanese manufacturers? While impatience at such restrictions is an element of the back-bench support of all governments to some degree, it has been particularly marked with the Labour administrations of the past fifty years, because of the expectations of radical reform held by supporters; 1924, 1929, 1945, 1964 – in each case there has been disappointment at the extent and the pace of change.

Disputes and rebellions, when they do occur, tend to focus on a particular decision or a particular policy. There are two reasons why this should be so: because opportunities to debate ideological values tend to be few (even the revisionist debates in the Labour Party centred as much around defence as the

Constitution of the Party itself). And secondly because, being specific, policy proposals are more open to specific criticism on grounds of ineffectiveness (that the programme will not in fact achieve the aims on which the Party is agreed, for example criticisms of resale price maintenance in the Conservative Party), inappropriateness (that the proposal is not an appropriate means of obtaining desired ends, for example the incomes policy of the Labour Government, or the reimposition of prescription charges), or unacceptability (disagreement over the aims of the policy itself, e.g. the refusal of the Conservative leadership to embrace the cause of the rebel regime in Rhodesia was not acceptable to some Conservative back-benchers, just as the re-establishment of German armed forces was not acceptable to some Labour supporters who were opposed to re-arming German troops, even within NATO).

In turn, this leads to the question: in a political system which lacks the institution of the referendum, yet which is possessed of a government which professes to be responsive to public opinion, how can a party – in power or in opposition – discover what the electorate really thinks on controversial questions? On a broad policy of economic recovery, would they prefer increases in direct, or indirect, taxation? Import controls, or devaluation? A reduction in social services, or in road-building? On dealing with Rhodesia, how far would there be public support for government measures: as far as the 'Tiger' concessions? Further than this? Would they accept armed intervention? Stronger United Nations sanctions? On paying for the rising costs of the National Health Service, does the public prefer paying prescription charges as an alternative to an increase in the weekly stamp? Without delving into the complicated question of how public opinion can be measured, communicated, or assessed in general, it could be said that in the British system there are three major substitutes for direct public voting on political questions, apart from indicators of opinion such as the Member of Parliament's post-bag, letters to the press, or demonstrations against government policy.

The first is the general election itself. It has been pointed out in an earlier chapter[8] that though in form this merely

⁸ See above, p. 60.

chooses 630 representatives of localities to sit in the House of Commons, in effect, because every serious candidate is affiliated to a major party, it is a method of choosing a party government. These parties put out election manifestoes, which, together with candidates' election addresses, speeches, television and radio broadcasts, posters, policy statements, press conferences, etc., tend to make the election a choice between collections of general policies. Thus the successful party, irrespective of the size of its parliamentary majority, or the possibility that it may have polled well under 50 per cent of the total vote (or, even, fewer votes than one of its rivals) will claim a mandate from the electorate to put through its proposed programme. This mandate theory has been criticized, particularly on the grounds that it does not act specifically – i.e. a majority may be against steel nationalization, yet may have preferred the Labour Party to the Conservative Party as a government. In what sense can they be said to have given a mandate for such a policy? On the other hand, policies not forecast in the election may be introduced by the government, in which case there is a readiness on the part of the opposition to point out that the government lacks any mandate to act: such was the case over the Conservatives' application to join the European Community. So, if the election is a substitute for direct public voting on issues, it is a very crude and uncertain one.

What, then, of pressure-groups? Can it be said that they transmit the opinions of the public on particular issues? To some extent this may be so. On the issue of British entry into the EEC groups were certainly very active on both sides, as was the press for a time. At the beginning of the century the tariff issue also attracted crowds, groups, spokesmen, publicity and money to both sides of the question. Comprehensive education, Rhodesian independence, and racial integration are other recent questions of great public concern in which groups have played a noticeable part in reflecting the various opinions of the public. But on other issues groups have tended to be found only on one side, and this can hardly be said to be indicative of the state of public feeling on the policy concerned: nuclear disarmament, the war in Viet-Nam, apartheid in South Africa, as well as more specialized issues such as more pay for certain occupations, the level of student grants, the cancellation of aircraft orders by the Government, or the Stansted airport issue. Here the conflict has tended to be one of group *v.* government, with those favouring the policies of the Government not seeing the necessity to organize in support of their view, except in extreme cases (as the pro-Gaullists did in France during the crisis of June 1968). Further, on many vital issues there may be little or no *organized* public opinion at all – over taxation changes for instance, or foreign policy matters, or alterations in the administration of the social services. Because of their complexity, or their lack of news value, only the parties, or groups concerned with particular specialized interests (e.g. members of occupations or owners of property affected by these policies) will become involved in discussion of the questions. So, if group action is a substitute for direct public voting on issues, it is a very partial and imprecise one.

The third alternative is the opinion poll. These – at least the best of them – tend to be quite accurate in obtaining replies to important questions or opinions concerning the popularity of the government or the Prime Minister, or the importance of certain issues as priorities. Despite occasional professions of contempt for, or indifference to, their messages, it seems probable that ministers and leading politicians do pay attention to the trends they indicate. By taking a careful sample, the polling organizations can claim that the results *do* show the state of public opinion on particular questions. But there are two major criticisms of polls as referenda substitutes. First, the selection of questions is left to the polling organizations, or their clients who sponsor the surveys. There is thus a temptation to select issues for investigation that are especially controversial or suited to press publicity or the special needs of the sponsor. So opinion on more mundane issues, yet issues which are nevertheless of considerable public importance, may not be investigated. Secondly, the organizations are private concerns, with no public responsibility other than that of their professional ethics. This means that there is no public check on the framing of the questions, the selection of samples, etc., and thus in the end polling can only be an indication of public opinion within its own limits, not a substitute for a direct referendum. Nor, in the same connection, is there the same public responsibility associated with responses as there is at an election or a referendum. It must also be remembered that the time element is important. An opinion poll is a snapshot, a static reflection of opinion, not a film of its dynamic state, and thus a series of polls is necessary in order to appreciate a trend in opinion. So, if the opinion poll is a substitute for direct public voting on issues, it is a very incomplete one.

Experience of the referendum in Europe and in some of the states of the USA has emphasized its limitations and its difficulties. It has been used in de Gaulle's France (e.g. to allow for the direct election of the President, or, in 1969, to effect certain alterations in the constitutional powers of the Senate and other institutional changes), and de Gaulle proposed its use to try to calm down the political fever of the 1968 crisis (but a general election was held instead). Some Swiss cantons use it, in accordance with the Swiss traditions of direct democracy. It is used in certain American states for a variety of matters, e.g. to alter the constitution of the state, to change certain laws which have been petitioned against by a requisite number of citizens (if a majority votes to change them), or to approve bonds issued to finance public works.

The main criticisms of its use are, first, that the questions are often complicated, and difficult to express briefly or in terms of a simple choice of approval or disapproval. Because many citizens who turn up at the polling station to vote for candidates for office are not prepared to struggle through the cumbersome paragraphs of perhaps a dozen or more proposals, voting on these issues tends to be low, and so the vote often cannot be regarded as an accurate reflection of popular opinion on the issue. Secondly, many of the questions, at least in the American states, are promoted or supported by interest-groups, who spend large amounts of money on campaigns to secure a favourable vote. This may well mean that no group or party bothers to put the opposing case, and the proposal carries, almost by default. While there may be a case for the referendum on strictly constitutional issues, its use on important policy questions detracts from party responsibility, while its use on unimportant questions arouses insufficient interest to make it a worthwhile exercise, even in conjunction with elections to office, as in California, for instance.

In May 1968, in a speech on the growth of violence in politics, the Minister of Technology, Anthony Wedgwood Benn, suggested that the apparent demand by the electorate for greater participation in decision-making might require the adoption of the referendum in British politics. Certainly, as the Minister mentioned in passing, technical methods of push-button voting in each household would soon be feasible, if rather costly. Whether such an institution would be desirable, in view of the criticisms that have been made of the referendum in other states, is another matter. Those who criticized the idea on the grounds that it would have unsettling repercussions on all our other political institutions – Parliament, the parties, Whitehall, local government – have a strong case. On the other hand, the increase in the scope of government functions, the pressure of legislative business in Parliament, the growing demands of Welsh and Scottish nationalism for greater autonomy, unrest in the Universities, apathy and frustration in the unions, the delicacy of many important political questions such as racial integration and immigration – the problem is grave, and perhaps radical methods to cope with these radical demands are the only solutions left?

GROUPS AND POLICY

Questions of political values and their expression do not only exist for political parties. Groups also have internal disputes over decision-making, the methods of policy-formation, and the basic values they seek to achieve. Indeed, for some groups, particularly those associated with some ethical position or philosophical value within the political system (such as pacifism, total abstention from alcoholic beverages, Sunday observance, white racial superiority), compromise is often regarded as betrayal, and the achievement of goals is seen as secondary to the means by which they are pursued. In this sense, they can be termed 'anti-Machiavellian' – the means of politics being more important than the ends.

In the nineteenth century, there can be found several familiar examples of such disputes. The Chartists, frustrated by the lack of early progress towards any of their 'six points', and with a feeling of resentment that the parliamentary reform of 1832 had done nothing to benefit the working-class, divided over the use of physical force to achieve their goals. Some abhorred the idea of using violence, others embraced it gladly, while many others took up positions between these extremes. Soon the divisions within Chartism over this question came to absorb so much of the attentions of its supporters that the movement itself was weakened. The Irish nationalists were divided over the same problem: whether to work through constitutional means or through violence. At the turn of the century, the suffragette movement contained many factions, each seeing the fight for the franchise as contributory to some larger struggle: socialism, the class war, feminism, democracy, and so on. Differences in aims led to differences in strategy. To some, an alliance with the new Labour Party was the most promising route to success; to others, it was essential to preserve an all-party appeal, either out of distaste for socialism, or out of recognition that it was unlikely that a Labour government would exist for many years to come.

Similar problems have beset more recent interest groups and political movements. The General Strike (1926) revealed the disparity between the values and goals of the ordinary trade-unionist, and those of the more revolutionary strikers who wished to proceed from general strike to revolution. The trade-unions have recently begun to question the value of their automatic alignment with the Labour Party, in view of its incomes policy and its proposals for trade-union legislation. The Campaign for Nuclear Disarmament not only contained conflicting factions over the strategies to be adopted in pursuing its aims (industrial action, propaganda programmes, marches and demonstrations, etc.), but also over the issue of how important was achievement of some measure of disarmament, compared to style, i.e. the uncompromising struggle against nuclear armaments irrespective of the possibilities of success. Such examples could be multiplied – the various elements of the student power movement, the policies of different sections of the medical profession before and after the establishment of the National Health Service,[9] and arguments within various white-collar trade-unions such as

[9] See the study by H. Eckstein, *Pressure-Group Politics* (Allen & Unwin, 1960).

NALGO and the teachers' organizations over membership of the Trades Union Congress.

Such internal conflicts arise from two basic causes: first, because there is a genuine dispute concerning the translation of agreed fundamental values into policies of a more specific form (e.g. will membership of the TUC *really* benefit the interests of the membership of the National Union of Teachers? Would co-operation with the National Health Service be more likely to preserve and enhance the status of the medical profession than a policy of non-co-operation?); second, because a particular policy or strategy is common to several groups with different ultimate aims and values: the Campaign Against Racial Discrimination for 'liberals' and for more radical supporters of something approaching black power, the Campaign for Nuclear Disarmament for outright pacifists as well as for moderates who distrust as ineffective or wasteful defence policies which are based on nuclear weapons. So the benefit of analysing group disputes in terms of the value-systems of the several factions is again apparent, for unless questions about their *ultimate* goals and values are raised, the problem may be seen merely as one of differences of interpretation rather than of incompatibility.

Again, the institutional arrangements and organizational 'style' of the group will have their influence. If a group is effectively controlled by a small number of individuals with a wide measure of agreement on the basic values they seek to achieve (e.g. the lobby for a foreign government, or a specialized industrial interest-group such as the motor-vehicle manufacturers or the oil refiners) then it is probable that their ideology, their policy and their specific decisions will all reflect their consensus. If a group is organized on the basis of representation of a variety of views, then conflict over means is almost guaranteed, and such disputes may escalate into conflict over basic values. These conflicts may reflect different political party affiliations (e.g. Communists and Labour supporters within a trade union) or different basic attitudes, for example on the basis of occupation (as with the various groups represented in the British Medical Association: specialists, senior and junior hospital staff doctors, general practitioners, etc.).

DEMOCRACY AND VALUES

Democracy multiplies the chances and opportunities of dissent and so limits the extent to which an identity of views can be achieved. Usually, therefore, the decisions it produces are heavy with compromise among divergent interests and opinions. Ideology, on the other hand, spurns compromise and in a high degree demands an identity of views and unanimity of purpose. In a democratic context this demand is likely to lead to continual controversy and an inability to make lasting decisions.[10]

This quotation sets out a dilemma of democratic political systems: how to obtain something of the purposefulness and direction of autocratic or totalitarian systems, while still preserving the freedom of choice, the freedom of expression and the freedom of dissension from official goals which are associated with representative popular government.

The same dilemma is posed for political organizations, whether parties or interest-groups, if run on democratic lines. Usually there are important underlying values which motivate the activities of members of these organizations, but also there are occasions when disagreement over these values will obstruct, and perhaps completely disrupt, the work of the group. Thus the Conservative Party generally manages to give a more positive appearance of unity than the Labour Party for two reasons: it is less ideological, being more inclined to the preservation of the status quo, and it is more autocratic in the sense that there is less demand for, and less self-consciousness about, opportunities for democratic decision-making. Thus there is less likelihood of disagreement over basic values arising in the first place. This greater degree of unity is probably a feature of moderate centre-parties when opposed by radical parties in any political system (the Gaullists in France and the CDU in West Germany are other examples).

It is certain that ideology is here to stay, in the sense that all social collectivities will possess or develop a set of basic values that will, explicitly or implicitly, act as guiding principles for their activities and behaviour. They may not be very specific; there may be considerable argument over their interpretation; they may not appear to have much obvious

[10] S. Beer, *Modern British Politics*, p. 239.

relationship to the ends that the group pursues; they may be modified considerably over time; but they can usually be traced by observation of how the group behaves and how it accounts for its behaviour. A group may claim to be non-ideological in the sense that it does not set out to achieve a series of radical policies in accord with a set of ideas – such as the primacy of the Aryan race, the Kingdom of Heaven on Earth, or the dictatorship of the proletariat – but it will turn out on examination to possess certain shared values. Of course, these values might include the acceptance of things as they are in preference to the unknown qualities of things as they might be, or the preference for dealing with problems as they arise, in their immediate context, rather than according to a set of radical aims applied regardless of context.

Ideology, in the sense used here, is also of value to the electorate, responsible as it is for making periodic choices between two or three political parties, or wishing to understand the aims of the multitude of interest-groups that are mentioned in the press or on television or radio programmes, and which clamour for public support. Ideology is a simplifying concept, so that decisions do not have necessarily to take the form of complicated choices between competing leaders and policies; instead they can take the form of the choice between continuing or terminating the support of a party whose basic values one has tended to agree with, regardless of specific policy disagreements, over a period of years.

Values may, then, be summarized as providing the motivation for political action by groups, the fuel for the vehicle of their political behaviour. On the other hand, there exist certain constraints – the brakes on the vehicle – which also affect the ways in which political parties and interest-groups take part in British political life.

7 Constraints

> There is nothing in which the power of
> circumstances is more evident than in
> politics.
>
> DISRAELI

Many people have an unthinking faith in the political omnipotence of party governments. 'They' can do anything they want, when they want, how they want. 'We' can only vote them out of office every five years or so, and then only to replace them with another set of rather similar-looking politicians. The same view is held about pressure-groups, collectively or individually. 'The unions' or 'big business' or 'the powerful men in the City' or the 'newspaper owners' or sometimes vaguer entities such as 'the Catholic Church' or 'the public school network' or 'the Masons' are seen as hidden manipulators of policy and political information. Such beliefs have two purposes for the people who hold them: they provide scapegoats for political actions that they do not like, and do not understand, such as high taxation, travel restrictions, housing shortages, unemployment, or inconvenient strikes, and they also offer a simple explanation of what would otherwise be an over-complicated political world.

To some extent, these beliefs are fostered, sometimes quite benevolently, by the politicians themselves. To gain election, they promise what they would, but cannot, fulfil. To keep office, they attempt to create an image of power, of achievement, that is just that little bit larger than life. Successes are given maximum publicity; failures, whatever the cause, are glossed over and forgotten. When faced with a problem, the politician will almost of necessity have to simplify its causes to his public; perhaps, in doing so, he simplifies them also to himself. In any case, the result is that when, as so often happens, a problem arises from a complicated set of multiple causes, it is difficult for the politician to accept that there *are* limits to his omnipotence, for such limits must seem, in some way, a matter of personal failure. It is with these limits as they affect parties in and outside the government, and pressure-groups, that this chapter is concerned. Why could Harold Macmillan not get us into the Common Market? Why could not Harold Wilson keep his promise to bring down the illegal regime in Rhodesia quickly? Why have successive Chancellors of the Exchequer been unable to end our financial difficulties? They all had the power – in the sense that nobody else was in positions of authority to bring about these effects. But they lacked the power that enabled them to bring about the ends they desired, at costs they could accept. At a different level, what prevents trade unionists from using their majority in the Labour Party's decision-making institutions to gain, through Labour's majority in Parliament, an all-round pay increase of 10 per cent? What prevents millionaires from using their wealth to buy advertising time on commercial television for the Conservative Party, as they might for soap-powder or cat meat? The answer, in brief, is that constraints on the possible courses of political action open to politicians are numerous, and are important. Politicians are not omnipotent, even when they are absolute dictators, for time, resources and foreign power will limit their options. In a democratic political system, such constraints are greater than ever, for democracy is, in itself, a type of deliberate limitation of the possibilities of power.

The previous chapter examined the ways in which the values of groups provided for them the motivations for political action. Before going on to consider the ways in which different types of constraints restrict political action by groups, it is necessary first to introduce the idea of the political system, as this will make the relationship between groups, their motivations and constraints easier to follow.

A political system is a set of institutions, and the relationships or interactions between these institutions. Thus, in the United Kingdom, the electorate, parties, pressure-groups, Parliament, the Cabinet, the Civil Service, the Monarch and local government bodies are the major political institutions, and they interact with each other in a variety of ways. But a political system is set in an environment, and is open to the effects of this environment. Thus the electorate consists of people with social, religious, economic and cultural attitudes which may influence their political behaviour. The cabinet must take account of the economic system; the Foreign Office is concerned with overseas political systems; pressure-groups belong also to the economic and social systems, and so forth. Some of these influences can be illustrated by the diagram (Fig. 2).

Or, by analogy, these constraints can be regarded as resistances in an electric circuit, or obstacles to the flow of a river which hold it back, divert it, slow it up, and concentrate and diffuse its force just as the flow of political pressure can be held back, diverted, slowed, or concentrated and diffused.

Constraints are of many types, and no attempt will be made here to classify them on the basis of their nature. But it is helpful in bearing in mind the effects of constraints to review the major sources from which they arise. First, there are constraints which originate within the political party or the interest or pressure-group itself. Some of these have been considered when the organization of these institutions was discussed, others in the previous chapter about disputes over basic values or ideology. Secondly, there are constraints within the political system – from other institutions, for example. And thirdly, there are constraints which have their origin outside the political system, either in a different sub-system of the society (such as the economic system) or from another state.

Of course, these do not always act separately: life is rarely that simple, even in politics. In considering a particular policy or decision, it will usually be the case that two, or even all three of these sources will be having their effect at the same time. The item-by-item treatment of these constraints that now follows should not obscure the complicated nature of the interactions that in fact occur.

INTERNAL CONSTRAINTS ON GROUP ACTION

Even in an ideal world for group action, where a decision on policy taken by a political party, or a strategy of pressure embraced by an interest-group, met with no obstruction once it was undertaken, there would still be problems for groups arising from within their own organizations.

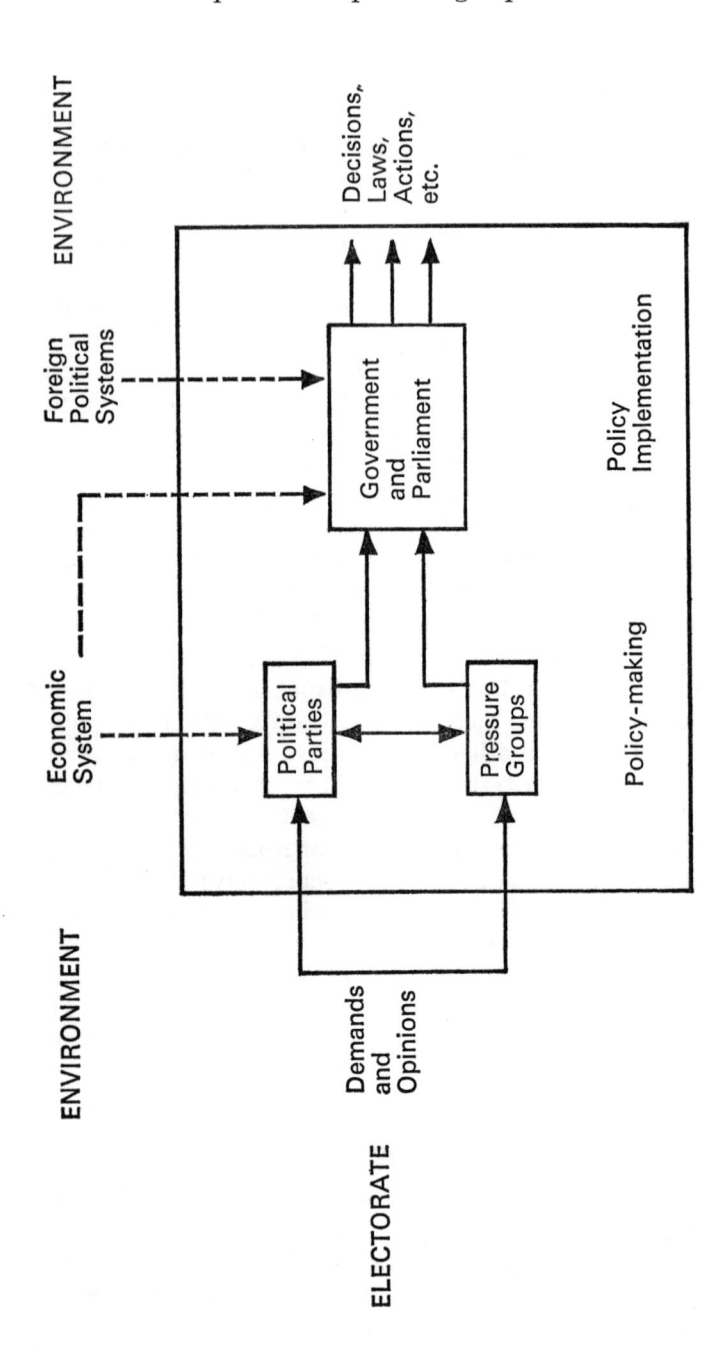

Fig. 2. The British Political System.

In the first place, organized groups – especially organized political groups – are rarely so harmonious that they avoid disputes concerning the disposition of resources available for use by the group. Even if agreement can be reached on the ends to which resources should be devoted, still there will arise conflicts over priorities for the allocation of resources. In this sense, of course, groups have their own 'politics', with perhaps their own 'political parties' and frequently their own 'interests' within the organization.

What are these resources that groups possess? Obviously money, or equivalent material items of value, springs first to mind. Money is almost a *sine qua non* for any organization, if only to pay for basic administrative needs – an office or headquarters, salaries for staff, postage and telephone bills, stationery, publications or communications to members, and so on. Beyond this, money is important to a group for two reasons. It widens the scope of available courses of action that the group can take in pursuit of its goals (it can pay for publications, advertisements, public meetings; it can subsidize educational functions such as conferences; it can buy research and surveys; on occasion, it can sponsor candidates for elections and support them if they are elected; it could even be used for illegal purposes such as bribery, if the group decided to undertake the risks involved!). It also enables the group to obtain substitutes for other resources it may lack – particularly time and organizational skills.

Time is often overlooked as a dimension and a constraint in politics. Yet it is the most inevitable of all limitations on political action. The Labour Party may wish, as the government of the day, to reform the House of Lords after its defiant rejection in June 1968 of the imposition of further sanctions against Rhodesia. Yet the party leadership is all the time aware that March 1971 is the very last month in which they can hold the next election. To draft the necessary legislation, to introduce it, to manœuvre it through the House of Commons and to allow for a possible year's delay because of rejection in the House of Lords would be a difficult undertaking in the time remaining before the next election. A pressure-group may wish to conduct a campaign against a Bill due to be introduced into the Commons in a few weeks' time. The shortage of time remaining available may well prevent the preliminary research being undertaken, the full discussion by members and the detailed planning of strategy by the leadership that would be desirable. Instead, a proposal has to be drafted, put to a hurriedly convened meeting of the membership, and set into operation on a hit-or-miss basis. Whether one is talking about the Labour Party or a small interest-group, the Conservatives or a trade union of a few hundred local workers, the Confederation of British Industries or a constituency Liberal Party worried about losing its deposit at the next election, time is of the essence, and a motto for all of them might be 'better an imperfect decision now, than a perfect decision tomorrow', if tomorrow is in any case too late.

Wealth and time are potential weapons for group political action, the shortage of which will limit what it is possible for a party or pressure-group to achieve. But their potential will go unrealized, and their scarcity will restrict even more severely the possibilities of group action, if the third type of resource is also unduly limited – the organizational skills which groups require. It is not easy to enumerate or classify these skills, and even if it were possible to list them, each group in any case would require a different 'mix' of the elements involved. But one obvious skill is leadership, and many groups are known to the public through the brilliance or notoriety of their leaders – the parties are often identified as much by the image of their Leaders as by their policies or principles; the TUC was George Woodcock until his retirement recently; the Transport Workers' Union was Frank Cousins, CND was Russell, Collins and Schoenmann, the Rhodesian lobby is Sandys and Lord Salisbury, the international student protest movement was associated variously with 'Danny the Red', Rudi Dutschke and Tariq Ali, among others. In any case, styles of leadership vary, and while one group may require inspiration from its Leader, another may want a conciliator, and a third may need a Leader prepared to give direction to the efforts of the group. What is important is that there should be leadership, and that it should be of a style suited to the needs of the group. Without leadership a party will be ineffectual, a pressure-group will be ignored.

Of the many other organizational skills that could be

mentioned, three of the most fundamental are those of planning, communication, and administration (including financial control). Planning is important, to take advantage of the time factor. It involves an appreciation of the resources available, including time, and the realization of the best way of combining the use of these resources in advance in order to achieve the goals on which the group is agreed. In a parliamentary campaign, for instance, it is important to know at what legislative stage the Bill will be most vulnerable, at what point press releases should be sent out, when MPs are most likely to be available to meet group supporters lobbying against the Bill. Planning, in other words, is the skill of combining resources, within the limitations of such constraints as exist, to the best advantage of the group and the achievement of its aims. To the extent that the planning function is overlooked or unavailable, group effectiveness is limited, whatever the other resources at hand.

The skill of communication can be appreciated by using the analogy of the human body. A body may be strong, and capable of powerful actions through its muscular system. It may contain a brain which is clever, able to plan and to appreciate the importance of significant events. But unless the nervous system is able to send messages quickly and accurately to all parts of the body, and to transmit back to the brain information about the actions which the body is carrying out, neither physical power nor mental cunning will be of any benefit. With a political party or pressure-group, the parallel holds. The most skilful leadership, together with the wealth and power provided by a large membership, are only of significance to the extent that the leaders and the members can communicate with each other swiftly and precisely. Such communication need not imply a democratic form of organizational control: it may be utterly authoritarian, as with an efficient military formation. It need not imply 'rationality': many fanatical groups have possessed efficient communications systems. But to the degree that the passing of commands, requests and information to the membership and the operating officials of the group, and the feedback of their replies and situation-reports, are impaired, so will the activities of the group be constrained. Such impairment may arise from insufficient channels of communication, or their overload by too many messages being passed along at any one time, or the channels may be too complicated for messages to move quickly or accurately. In the struggle between the Gaullists and the Communists for supremacy in the liberation of Paris from the Germans, a message was sent from the Gaullists to the Communists inviting them to join an attack on the Prefecture of Police the next day. The internal communications system of the Communists was so complicated (for security reasons) that the message reached their leaders too late for them to take part, and the Gaullists gained the building – along with the prestige and strategic advantage that went with it![1]

Administration is the third skill that may be in short supply in an organization. Under this heading is included also the ability to manage the financial resources of the group to its best advantage. The General Secretaryship of the Labour Party, the Chairmanship of the Conservative Party, the leading administrative offices of pressure-groups have all been recognized as key positions, as vital in their own way to the exercise of successful political power as the leadership itself. Involved in administration are the co-ordination of activities, the operation of plans, the management of personnel – in fact the donkey-work necessary to turn ideas into action, plans into realities, proposals into achievements. With poor administration, work will run behind schedule, budgets will be overspent, messages delayed even if proper communication facilities are available, and disorganization will obstruct the careful appreciation of past activities on which future plans can be based. To the demagogue, to the leader over-concerned with speeches and ideals, administration may be seen as 'mere management'. To the Member of Parliament, or the Minister, or the pressure-group leaders concerned to steer a Bill through Parliament, or the party officials trying to maximize the impact of the party's efforts for the next election, administration will be recognized as one of the major political skills.

Shortages of the resources of money, time and skills are relative – what may be adequate for one group may be insufficient for another, what may be sufficient for the achievement

[1] L. Collins and D. Lapierre, *Is Paris Burning?* (Penguin, 1966), p. 108.

of one or two limited goals may be inadequate for the attainment of a complicated programme of aims. So, irrespective of the availability of resources, at any one time it is likely, particularly in the case of political parties, that resources will not be plentiful enough to satisfy all the demands of members at the same time. So parties, and many pressure-groups, will be faced with the problem: how do we allocate, over time, the money and skills possessed by the group, to these priorities? How, indeed, do we decide on priorities? It is over these questions that most internal disputes in groups will occur, provided that there is agreement over basic values. Even if there is no such agreement, in an ideological dispute control over priorities and allocation (through control of the leadership and other decision making elements of the group) is an important weapon. For the Labour Party, such priorities may concern, say, economic recovery or social reform, and, within these categories, questions of specific priorities: incomes policy or export incentives? Regional development or transport reorganization? Educational reform or a new system of local government? For the Conservatives, planning for their return as the governing party, the basic question might be: new programmes, or the repeal of the Labour Government's legislation which the Conservatives have opposed? For a railwaymen's or miners' union: the prevention of redundancy, or the improvement of the profitability of the industry? All the alternatives may be desirable to the group concerned. The scarcity of resources imposes constraints. Choices have to be made.

Political parties and most pressure-groups, being highly organized bodies, tend to rely upon a complex procedural system to expedite business and to contain as well as to prevent conflict. Yet such procedure is itself a constraint upon group action, in the same way as a Constitution – whether written or conventional – constrains the actions of governments, or the rules constrain players in a game. Within the limits of the rules of procedure, there may well be a considerable area of discretion, and this applies particularly to the party in power. But in many cases, especially those of most importance to group aims, swift responses to situations are prevented by the need to take decisions through the proper channels, and changes in the policies, procedures or values of a group often require lengthy consideration by many different parts of the organization. In the case of the Labour Party, for instance, a change in policy would require consideration by the parliamentary party, probably also by the National Executive Committee, and, if it was of a fundamental nature, by Conference as well. Major decisions by trade unions are taken mainly by their annual conference, with provision for emergency ballots of members by mail on some issues, such as the desirability of strike action. Procedure (though criticized as 'red tape' by those who are hampered by it from time to time) is a necessary part of organization, but since it has a protective function to prevent leaders and others from taking decisions irresponsibly, it is also very much a constraint on the range of courses of action available to a group, at least in the short-run.

CONSTRAINTS IMPOSED BY THE POLITICAL SYSTEM

Why does the Earth get pulled from its path into an orbit round the Sun? What prevents an athlete from increasing his metabolism sufficiently to run a three-minute mile? Why cannot the supplier of a product double the price of his goods in order to increase his profits? What prevents an efficient political party from carrying through its policies quickly and completely?

In each of these cases a complicated answer may be summarized in this form: each is constrained by the interactions of elements in a system. The Earth is subject to gravitational forces of the Sun and other celestial objects; the physiological system of the athlete constrains his heartbeat rate and muscle activity within certain critical limits; the existence of other suppliers restricts the price at which a producer can sell his goods; and the existence of other elements of the political system with their own patterns of behaviour and their own interests sets limits to what a political group can achieve.

The competition of other groups imposes many constraints on parties and on pressure-groups. A party in power is harassed by the opposition parties; it must devote some of its attention and much of its resources to matters other than the consideration of policy, and especially to electoral prospects. A pressure-group is a single voice in a clamorous crowd; much of its energy must be aimed at getting its message across, to the right targets, in the right manner, at the right place and at the right time. No sooner is a Minister persuaded by the case of group A, who *must* have a favourable Bill pushed through Parliament, than his attention is diverted by the pleas of group B, who are determined that no such Bill shall pass, and then comes the advocacy of group C, who want from the Minister something entirely different anyway. So the share of the Minister's attention, sympathies and efforts, the share of the resources of his department, the possible claim on the very limited time of Parliament and the Cabinet that any one of these groups can hope to command is likely to be much smaller than if the other groups had not existed; nor, in the British system, can they add emphasis to their requests in the way the venal pleaders in Gogol's tale of Czarist bureaucracy, *The Government Inspector*, could, with suitable bribes. Thus the Secretary of State for Education may listen sympathetically to the problems of the deputation from the National Union of Teachers, but the same day's appointments could include visits from representatives of local authority education departments, and a deputation from the National Union of Students or the National Association of Schoolmasters. Thus the force of the efforts of the first group of visitors is necessarily diluted.

Like the groups themselves, the political system has its procedures, and mastery of such procedures is one way a group can gain advantages over its competitors. The commercial television lobby, by its skill in using procedures rather than being hampered by them, was a good example of this. Nevertheless, the game of politics must be played by the rules that exist, and neither a political party nor a pressure-group will be active for very long before being frustrated by some aspect of procedure – a private Member's Bill being counted out for lack of a Friday quorum, a railway Bill in the nineteenth century being lost because it had not completed all its legislative stages before the end of the parliamentary session, a Liberal or a Labour government finding its legislation rejected by a Conservative-dominated House of Lords, a ministerial order favourable to a pressure-group being challenged in the courts. In these and many other ways procedures may prevent groups from getting all they want, when they want it.

The many limitations of the internal communications system of the group were seen to be constraints on actions by the group. Similarly, the communications capacity of the political system itself may impose restrictions on what political groups may achieve. In Britain, there is a wide range of media for carrying information and persuasive messages from groups to other elements of the political system: the public, Parliament, the cabinet, the departments, local government organizations. The mass media (the press, broadcasting, outdoor advertizing), the technical equipment of telecommunications, the postal service, a metropolitan centre offering facilities for lobbying, demonstrations, face-to-face discussion, committee meetings, and so forth, the chambers of Parliament itself – all these are available. Why, then, is it still possible to treat the communications system as a constraint as well as an opportunity?

In the first place, from the point of view of any single group – even that of a wealthy national political party – these media are busy. There is great competition for their use; it is often costly to use them; therefore the probability of a message not only being transmitted but being given sufficient saliency by the receiver is often not very high, at least within the limits of the group's budgetary allocation for any one purpose. What attention is given to a television election broadcast, in competition the same evening with, say, a national sporting event, a popular serial, carefully-prepared advertisements and a variety show? What impact does a half-page advertisement against nationalization have on a newspapers' readers? What can one, or a dozen, or a hundred letters to an MP achieve on behalf of a pending Bill, especially in view of the Member's attention to the party line?

Second, there is the problem of language. The style in which a case is presented in a speech by a sponsored MP to the House of Commons may be almost meaningless to the average television viewer. The bluster and bombast of the candidate seeking re-election must somehow be replaced by a more appropriate manner if he is to make his case to a meeting of the parliamentary party. Selection of language and terminology that is suited to the prospective audience is very much a constraint on action.

And thirdly, the question of target: what channels are most likely to reach the target of the message? It is not much use trying to arouse Labour supporters by advertising in the *Daily Telegraph*, or trying to persuade the Conservative leadership of one's case by means of a letter carried in the columns of the *Morning Star*. A mailed pamphlet from a pressure-group is likely to have little impact on the average Member of Parliament, if only because he receives so many, and his time and attention are too limited to devote to any one single item. The communications system thus constrains groups in their achievements by the selective attention given to various media by the different targets of political influence.

Another parallel constraint is that of the resources of the political system. Just as the limitation of wealth, time and skills available to the party, the lobby and the interest-group affected what they could achieve, so do similar scarcities within the political system as a whole. The money available to the government at any one time is limited; expansion of the money supply brings on the dangers of inflation, while to increase the government's share of the gross national product may well diminish the rate at which the national income grows in the future. So the government faces the same problems of allocation of resources as groups have to deal with. For example, the recurrent British financial crises mean that school building has to be cut back from its previously-planned levels. Representations from groups interested in educational policy are of little avail, however well presented they might be, for the question they cannot easily answer is this: if we give *your* proposals priority, what other social service expenditures would you reduce, to balance the extra costs? Time is also scarce, and the legislative programme for a parliamentary session is soon filled up. To left-wing MPs, thirsting for the abolition of the political power of the House of Lords, the question of time is put: if we give this proposal priority in our coming schedule, what other parts of the programme would you see postponed, in order to make the time available? The skills of leadership are scarce. To reformers welcoming the Report of the Fulton Committee on the Civil Service, and who wish to implement the recommendation that control of the service should be placed more immediately under the Prime Minister, the question is: what other business would you suggest receives less attention from him in future? Groups may well be bold enough to offer their answers to these questions, but if they do, they risk defensive action by groups which will be adversely affected by the changes.

The vulnerability of the political system itself to stress will force it to regulate group activity when this reaches levels dangerous to the survival of the system. The warnings of politicians in the past five years that the British electorate has had too much party activity, especially in the form of elections, is one sign of this. The ideas that were raised about 'all-party coalitions' or 'government by businessmen' during the devaluation crisis (1967) – on the grounds that party governments would not or could not govern in the best interests of the country – arose from a similar cause. The activities of the Mosleyites and the Communists in the 1930s were a clear instance of group activity endangering the continued existence of the British political system, and, since some of their politically dangerous activities were nevertheless legal, new laws more in keeping with social requirements were passed, such as the Public Order Act 1936 which restricted the wearing of uniforms and the holding of processions by political groups. The party 'truce' of the Second World War period can be regarded as a (voluntary) constraint accepted by the major parties in order not to prejudice the survival of the system when it was threatened by a major foreign war. Under normal circumstances, the strong political traditions and entrenched institutions of the British system enable it to tolerate, indeed to benefit from, quite alarming levels of party or pressure-group activity, even when it edges over into civil disobedience, or where it imposes temporary hardship on the public. Even the more self-consciously democratic United States system appears restrictive by comparison, and recent events in France and West Germany have demonstrated the fragility of their political systems when faced with high levels of political activity. But even in Britain, there is regulation by the government of the day when it seems that the context requires a limit to toleration; what may be acceptable in normal times may have to be proscribed in times of crisis, and such crises themselves may be the result of party or pressure-group activity. The state cannot accept the notion that there is a right of political expression that supersedes the survival of the system in which such expression can occur. The danger is that the government may use this necessity as a too-ready excuse for restrictions in its own partisan interests.

The last instance of a constraint imposed by the political system is an obvious one, but one easily overlooked by the planners and the strategists in party headquarters or the committee meetings of interest-groups. It is this: the political system is a *social* system, composed of humans organized in various ways. Because they are human, they are not only fallible and necessarily subjective in their outlook, they are also, at least part of the time, likely to behave irrationally. Therefore precise predictions of human behaviour may well turn out to be false simply because they were precise, because they did not allow for the irrational choice, the unthinking action, the selection of apparently senseless alternatives. Such irrationality, for instance, surprises party workers who find working-class Conservatives in council houses, or middle-class Socialists in Hampstead. It is found both within interest-groups and among the audiences they seek to influence. The persuasion campaigns that have been praised most highly have not been those that have presented a case most convincingly by the use of logic, but most persuasively by appeals to emotion as much as to reason. The major political parties have employed this appeal in their election posters and slogans ('Let's Go With Labour'; 'Life's Better with the Conservatives – Don't Let Labour Ruin It!'; 'If you think like a Liberal, vote like a Liberal'). The slogans and symbols of CND, student power movements, the anti-nationalization campaigns and the pirate radio campaign of a few years ago were also aimed at basically non-rational persuasion. This is not to say that any of these parties or groups lacked logical argument, only that they found occasions when, tactically, other types of argument seemed better. It is still valuable from time to time to revise the lessons of Graham Wallas' classic *Human Nature in Politics*, and recall his emphasis on instinct, habit and emotion as factors in human political behaviour.

CONSTRAINTS FROM OUTSIDE THE POLITICAL SYSTEM

Political activity is only one part of the sum of human behaviour. We have seen how parties and pressure-groups are limited in their choice of alternatives by factors arising from within their own organizations, and how they are constrained in various ways by aspects of the political system in which they operate. Now it is necessary to survey the residual category of constraints imposed either by other parts of the social system (such as the legal and economic systems), or by systems outside Britain altogether.

It is quite plain that options available to British parties and pressure-groups, in pressing for certain policies or trying to prevent the adoption of others, are limited by the decisions and actions of other political systems. In some cases, in some very important cases, these limitations operate at one remove, by acting on the British government, which is a party government. Thus the actions of an ally may involve Britain in a war on her side in support of treaty obligations, despite the preference of the party in power for peaceful settlement of the dispute, since the alternative, to disregard the treaty, may be a worse option. The decision of Ian Smith and his colleagues to declare unilateral independence, and their subsequent refusals to negotiate on British proposals, have restricted not only the possible actions of the Labour Party, but those of the opposition Conservative Party as well. Foreign economic policies can affect British politics and thus the choices open to British parties and pressure-groups; an American tax reduction or an increase in their level of import duties, the stability or otherwise of the French franc, the forcible nationalization of British assets in overseas countries – all these will shape the policies of British parties and groups interested in political activity.

With the exception now of the British Communist Party and student movements, and perhaps some instances of trade union activities, there is little evidence of direct constraints on British group activity by foreign organizations. The values, programmes and policies of British groups are on the whole indigenous. The remaining constraints that arise outside the political system itself are those which originate from other sub-systems of British society. In particular, the legal, economic and social-cultural sub-systems limit in a wide variety of ways the possibilities of group political action. The convenience of classification of these constraints as belonging to non-political sub-systems should not tempt one into neglect of their political effects. The legal system is concerned with the laws of the country, for example, but it is clear that the laws are passed in the first place by political institutions – the government and Parliament – generally for political purposes (to carry out policies, for example) – and they may well have political effects when they are in force.

There are many examples of laws which relate to political parties and pressure-groups quite directly. (Obviously the activities of political groups are also subject to the normal laws of the land, against fraud, violence, larceny, conspiracy, etc.). The laws which surround electoral practice in Britain certainly constrain the political behaviour of parties. The prohibition of various nineteenth century electoral practices by Acts of Parliament in 1868, 1872 and 1883[2] lessened reliance on bribery, corruption and violence. Limitation on expenditure under the Corrupt Practices Act, 1883, and the Representation of the People Acts, 1918 and 1948, meant that parties could not rely on swamping a constituency with costly advertising campaigns, nor carry hordes of electors to the polls in hired limousines. Voluntary persuasion and a thorough canvass became essential substitutes; the unpaid party worker became much more valuable. Other examples of legal constraints are: restrictions on the times, places and methods of public assembly (the law, dating back to 1817, forbidding demonstrations within the environs of Parliament when it is in session, is a case in point), the laws of libel and slander, the times and methods of balloting (especially the secrecy of the vote), the legal qualifications necessary for nominations, and those that must be possessed by candidates and the voters, the rules of parliamentary privilege, which may affect parties and pressure-groups alike, and the latest constraint, the necessity for disclosure in the balance-sheet of any sizeable donations by companies to political causes.

[2] C. O'Leary, *The Elimination of Corrupt Practices in British Elections* (Oxford University Press, 1962).

Social and cultural constraints, though less clear-cut than legal constraints, and with a different set of sanctions for their breach, still exercise considerable influence over the 'what' and 'how' of politics. Just as much as legal restrictions, so social restrictions vary from country to country. What is regarded as right and proper business for a political party to engage itself with in one state may be thought highly improper in another. The influence of the Roman Catholic Church in Italian politics through various political organizations such as 'Catholic Action' and the Christian Democratic Party itself would be regarded with great suspicion and mistrust in the British context. The concern of British politics with problems of recreation and the arts would be considered, in other countries or in Britain in an earlier period, an example of improper political meddling in social matters.

It is true that in nearly all states in the modern world the limits of acceptability of political concern in social and cultural matters have widened, and the dividing-lines between the political and non-political have become less sharp. But some things are still regarded in Britain as being outside the concern of politics and politicians (and there are some who, mistrusting political means of lessening social tension or ameliorating social problems, would extend this category considerably!). Matters of religious faith, for example, are not seen as susceptible to political intervention, so that it is still legal for a patient, out of religious faith, to refuse, at risk of his life, certain forms of medical treatment such as blood transfusions. Yet it is not open to a parent to keep a child from school on religious grounds, or to a taxpayer to withhold taxes, or disregard road signs when travelling in a car. Other matters may be regarded as properly decided by our political institutions, yet there are social conventions against them becoming issues of party policy: generally matters relating to social behaviour (divorce, recreation, reform of family law) or the penal code (abolition of the death penalty, for example).

Such restraints on party policy do not apply with the same force to pressure-groups. It is seen as quite legitimate for groups to attempt to influence Parliament for or against the merits of reforming the law on homosexuality, for example, or the abolition of judicial corporal punishment, or on religious questions. This difference arises from the nature of parties and pressure-groups; pressure-groups are generally primarily concerned with social or cultural matters, and politics is only one means among many that they can use to achieve their ends. To a political party, politics is its full-time concern.

The problem of the limits of political action on religious questions is not quite as delicate in Britain as it might be on occasion in, say, the United States of America. In part, this may be due to the establishment of state religions in both England and Scotland; in part, because of the presence of the Bishops and Archbishops in the House of Lords, to speak on behalf of the Anglican Church in particular, and the Christian churches in general. This gives a freedom and a legitimacy to political discussion of religious matters that might not occur if reform of the House of Lords abolishes religious representation as such. On the other hand this is (with the membership of the House of Lords afforded to the 'law lords') a type of functional representation which, rather unfairly, is not extended to the non-established denominations. The Methodist Donald Soper is only Lord Soper; but Donald Coggan is Archbishop of York.

The constraints from the economic system stem from the problem of scarce resources. However powerful a political party might be when acting as the government, however much influence a pressure-group may command, their demands are not only affected by the money available to their own organizations and to the government, (which constraints have been discussed earlier in this chapter) but also the resources available to society as a whole. If total national income declines, it is likely that the product of taxation will also decline. Indeed, unemployment benefit and similar claims on social services in a time of depression may place severe stresses on the political system, as happened in 1930–1. This explains why Mr Wilson put the problems in these terms in 1964:

> Why do we give such a high priority to expanding production? The answer is that all else in our programmes and our vision for the new Britain depend on what we turn out from our factories, mines and farms; our laboratories and our drawing offices.

Such phrases have become more frequent in recent years, as

politicians of all parties have recognized that reforms, expansion of social services, the development of education programmes, reductions in taxation and other priorities depend on economic growth.

The problem of communication has been labelled a constraint both internally (communication within the party or the pressure-group) and from the political system (the limitations of political communication in the political system). It is also an important constraint arising from the need to communicate with other states and with other social sub-systems of British society. The language problem is at best a delay, at worst an almost insuperable handicap on the actions of parties and groups interested in, or affected by, events in foreign countries, the Viet-Nam war, riots in Paris, the Russian economy, the Greek coup, Czechoslovakia's 'new course', civil war in Nigeria, the Arab-Israeli dispute – all these situations are reported in the various languages of the countries concerned. While English-speaking reporters will send their despatches to their papers or broadcasting station, these reports will be edited down to a few hundred words at most for release to the public. So how can the Conservative Party, or relief organizations, or the TUC, or friendship organizations, obtain a fuller appreciation of events? In the main, by reading reports in the language concerned, which imposes the delay of translation, if translation can be afforded. Such delay may be critical if the aim is, say, to forestall government action, for the government has priority for receiving reports and skilled translators in the civil and foreign services to provide summaries of information with speed.

The language problem involved in dealing with the legal, economic and social sub-systems is more subtle. Each has its own brand of English, its jargon, which the politicians may misunderstand. The Latin tags and wordy precision of the lawyer, the arcane concepts of the economist, the strange phraseology of the sociologist, all impose their own translation problem on the practising politician. The judge may appear perverse in refusing to look at the words of the Minister or the debate on the Bill in Parliament when confronted with the problem of interpreting a statute. The warnings of the economist concerning the balance of payments, the incidence of taxation, or the effects of regional unemployment may seem carping to the party spokesman eager to see his party in office. The academic discourse of the social scientists, analysing problems of family poverty, or race relations, or life in the new towns, may seem too detached and passionless to the Member of Parliament concerned with a specific problem from his constituency, or the demonstrators of a hastily organized pressure-group aroused by a newspaper report of a politician's speech on immigration. The reverse problem, that of explaining to representatives of these other sub-systems the problems of the politician in language which *they* can understand, is also important.

CONSTRAINTS AS OPPORTUNITIES

The long recital of constraints on political action which has made up this chapter is daunting, but it is also, from another aspect, a charting of opportunities of which the skilful, the enthusiastic, the well organized group can take advantage. Like the sonnet form or the 'haiku' to the poet, the rules of the game to the cricketer or bridge-player, the chart of difficult sea-passages to the yachtsman, the constraints and limitations of the political situation allow the fittest party or pressure-group not only to survive, but to thrive. Constraints are not so much obstacles to politics as the stuff of politics. The early campaigns of Senator Eugene McCarthy in 1968 demonstrate how lack of money and organizational skills can be turned into an advantage, so that the campaign of the underdog in New Hampshire and later primaries became a snowballing crusade proud of its distinctive amateur style. The deftness of the skilled Parliamentarians (Bevan, Silverman, Hogg, Grimond) shows how a knowledge and understanding of procedural limitations can become a weapon rather than a burden. The more experienced among the lobbyists know how to use the constraints of the system to gain their ends, even when a powerful government, possessing a skilled bureaucracy in Whitehall and a strong majority in Westminster, would rather deny the group its claims than grant them. Public opinion, fear of bad publicity, the idea of representative democracy can constrain governments as well as pressure-groups.

All this is not to say that such constraints are immutable.

The group may increase its resources, and improve its internal communications; it may achieve a more favourable position in the political system (e.g. the change in the TUC's role over the past fifty years, or the rise of the Labour Party); it may improve its relationships with external sub-systems e.g. by winning to its ranks experts in law or economics. The constraints themselves may change by political action – think how much advantage the Liberals or the Nationalist parties would gain from proportional representation, or certain pressure-groups from functional representation in a second chamber, or all the parties from some form of governmental subsidy such as that given the West German parties for political education purposes. The parties and the pressure-groups themselves are aware of the possibilities of favourable and unfavourable change, remembering Machiavelli's maxim in *The Prince* that 'one change always leaves the path prepared for the introduction of another'. It is the mark of a skilful politician that he can take advantage of change in the constraints and opportunities of his society.

8 Groups and the political system: comparison and contrast

To highlight some of the major aspects of the behaviour and structure of British political groups, this chapter deals with some comparative aspects of political parties and pressure-groups, using illustrations from other political systems.

The emphasis of this comparative survey is on the effects which the structure and the values of the political system as a whole can have on the behaviour of parties and groups, and in particular how each of four types of political systems requires that certain special functions are performed by parties and groups. These four categories are:

(i) *Open systems*, which permit and, indeed, encourage influences from other systems in society and from foreign political systems to be taken into account in the determination of policy.

(ii) *Closed systems* prohibit, as far as possible, such influences from affecting policy, and deny to all but permitted institutions any access to policy-making organizations (censorship, control of religious, economic and social groups by the state, restrictions on foreign travel are marks of a 'closed system').

(iii) *Divided systems*, which may be either open or closed, have as one of their major political problems the task of integrating divisive elements into the system, and parties and pressure-groups may both reflect the divisions, and aid in the integrative processes, of such a system (Nigeria, Canada and Cyprus are examples).

(iv) *Developing systems* have as their overriding political concern the establishment of political authority and national identity at a time when the state is passing through a phase of economic and social upheaval, in many cases following the achievement of independence (almost any state but South

Africa would offer an African example, almost any state but Japan an Asian example).

These categories are not, of course, either absolute or exclusive. States have relatively open or closed systems, though they may tend to cluster towards the extremes of this dimension, but Britain is more open than France, post-coup Greece than the USSR, the USSR than China. Similarly, divided systems may be – as most states are to some extent – 'developing' politically, and may be relatively open or closed as well.

Of course, there are problems in attempting to compare other types of political system with that of Britain. Various differences of history, language, culture and political organization prevent naïve comparisons of party with party, group with group, from being of very much value. For example, the political role of the TUC in Britain is significantly different from that of one of the French federations of trade unions, which have a more ideological commitment to Catholicism, Socialism, Communism or mild radicalism, and is totally unlike anything that is done politically by the trade unions of Soviet Russia. Or, if we start from the functions that parties perform in Britain, rather than their structures, we find that many of these are performed in other countries by quite different agencies: thus opposition in the German Federal Republic has relied more on the press and student activism in the past two years than on the only non-coalition party still represented in the Bonn Parliament – the Free Democrats – though the outcome of the 1969 federal elections means that a major party – the CDU – is once more responsible for the task of opposition; a legal, commercial or administrative background is a more probable route to the White House in the USA than a legislative career of party orthodoxy such as is prescribed for would-be residents of 10 Downing Street; interests and localities influence legislators far more than does party discipline in the USA, while it is the party rather than the interest-group that dominates the decisions of British Members of Parliament.

But comparative analysis can be helpful as well. The very fact that differences of function are discovered by comparative study emphasizes the importance of parties in the cases under comparison and the fact that certain general political functions tend to be performed within a system if not by one agency then by another. Comparisons may reveal trends in development, for example from a multi-party to a two-party system under certain conditions, or the tendency for a newly-independent state to gravitate towards a one-party system, or the conditions which pre-dispose a political system to military coups.[1] The very features of parties or pressure-groups in a state which a native observer perhaps takes for granted or overlooks altogether may have their importance underlined by careful comparison with parties or groups in other systems. So, handle comparative analysis with care, avoid the assumption that a literal translation of a word implies the precise translation of a political attribute ('democracy' east and west of the iron curtain, 'cabinet' in English and French, 'Secretary of State' in the British, United States and West German governmental systems, for example) and make allowance for the dissimilarities in a system which differences in geography, history and culture will have produced, and comparison can be of great value.

GROUPS AND THE STRUCTURE OF THE POLITICAL SYSTEM

The previous chapter of the book was concerned with the constraints which shaped or restricted the choices which groups might make regarding their courses of action. Among these constraints were several of a constitutional nature, that is to say they derived from legal or conventional rules of the political system itself. But while such rules – the arrangements by which the political system is run – are important in considering *what* choices are available to groups, it is wise to remember that they also affect the pattern of parties and pressure-groups which already exist, in other words *which* groups take part in the politics of a particular state.

Examples of such influences on the structure of the system could be drawn from almost any developed polity, and from several of the so-called underdeveloped or the traditional polities as well. It is preferable, therefore, to consider certain aspects of the constitutional arrangements of states, and find

[1] S.Finer, *Man on Horseback* (Pall Mall, 1962) deals comparatively with the intervention of the military in the politics of various states.

examples to illustrate them, rather than to undertake a world tour, state by state.

Probably the best-known – though still extremely controversial – case is that of the relationship between the electoral system used in a state, and the number and types of political parties which are found in the political system. In particular, states which possess some form of proportional representation as their electoral system are believed to be more likely to include a multiplicity of parties, and parties which frequently change their names, composition, policies and alliances, than states which have a British-type system of single-member constituency voting. The crude evidence for this is to contrast the two-party system of Britain (with certain exceptional periods such as the inclusion of the Irish Party from the 1880s to 1918, and the Liberal-Labour struggle for the position of chief opposition party in the 1920s) with the multi-party systems of Weimar Germany and the Third and Fourth French Republics. This connection between single-member constituencies and the two-party system has led the two major West German parties to consider revising the West German electoral system. (At present it is a mixture of direct elections, and proportional representation achieved by the addition of candidates from party lists). This change is intended to deprive the National Democratic Party in particular from any chance of representation, and to lessen the need for coalition governments in future.

But the relationship is not that simple. France has experimented with many types of electoral system in the present century (including its present single-member constituencies) but has always had a multiplicity of parties. Despite Germany's modified proportional representation system, there are only two major parties, and a third party which polls about the same percentage of votes as the British Liberal Party (though it has in consequence a larger share of parliamentary seats). Belgium, using a non-proportional system in the nineteenth century, and a proportional system in the twentieth century, experienced little change in the religious and regional basis of its party voting. Germany, using a system of single-member seats, elected more parties to the pre-1918 Parliament than ever she did under Weimar's much-criticized proportional system. Other factors besides type of electoral system have to be taken into account in explaining the number of parties of a state. If there is a series of deep, ideological, ethnic or regional divisions within a state, it is likely that the type of electoral system used will not have more than a marginal effect on the number of parties in existence. In some cases, a separate party will be the means of integrating certain elements of society into the political system (in Germany the Christian Socialists are a separate party, based on Bavaria, even though for most *political* purposes they act in the closest of alliances with the Christian Democrats at national level). History and the political culture of the state are factors at least as important as the electoral system in determining the identities of parties.

Federal systems may have an effect on party behaviour by separating administrative and legislative power, by emphasizing the local basis of members of the national legislature, and by increasing the importance of regional, rather than national, issues. While this is true to a minor extent in Canada (particularly for Quebec politicians), Nigeria before the coups and the subsequent civil war, and Switzerland, the most important example is the United States of America. Here nationally organized parties only go into action for the quadrennial presidential elections, and party discipline in the Congressional parties is weak, mainly because of a lack of sanctions which a party leader can exercise. True, patronage and committee assignments have some effect in persuading recalcitrant Senators or Congressmen to pay attention to party decisions, but renomination and re-election depend on the 'folks back home'. *Their* interests will have to be satisfied first, whether on an issue of tariffs, weapon procurement for the armed forces, labour laws, gun control, or conservation of natural resources. Franklin Roosevelt, one of the strongest of modern Presidents and supported by an overwhelming national vote in his 1936 re-election campaign, tried, by campaigning against them, to deny re-election to a number of Congressmen and Senators in 1938 who had been opposing his programme, but his few successes were more than compensated for by his spectacular failures. No President has tried overtly to impose his leadership in this way since then.

Other constitutional factors that affect the structure,

behaviour and relative power of parties include: the number of elective offices available for party competition (contrast the British system – concerned only with MPs and local councillors – with the USA, with its President, Vice-President, Senator, Representative, state legislator, municipal officers and representatives, Governor of the state, legal and administrative posts 'up for grabs' at various times); the relative independence of the executive and legislative branches of government (the British Prime Minister is much more intimately associated with the fortunes of his party than, say, the French or German President); and procedural arrangements such as whether elections are at fixed, pre-determined intervals or are open in their timing to the influence of the ruling party, on the British model, the rules governing the raising and spending of party finance, and the degree of influence or 'legitimacy' afforded to opposition parties by law (e.g. the salary paid to Britain's Leader of the Opposition, the transitional arrangements for presidential succession in the USA).

The political structure of states also affects pressure-groups in various ways. One aspect of structure of importance to pressure-groups is the extent to which political parties are disciplined by their leadership, for, if the penalties of voting against the party line are severe (and especially if, as in Britain, such rebellion may lead to the dissolution of Parliament) then the likelihood of pressure-groups winning over individual legislators rather than the party as a whole, is small. Where legislators are not so closely linked with the government, as in the USA, and to a lesser extent in France and West Germany, then their opportunities for successful influence over the making of legislation by pressure on the legislator increase. The degree of bureaucracy is another factor affecting groups. The more specialized and the more developed a civil service becomes in a state, the more it will be tempted to rely on pressure-groups for information and even assistance concerning their fields of interest, and, in consequence, the more likely it is that such aid will be rewarded by favourable treatment, consultation in advance of new legislation being proposed by the government, etc. Thus advanced and highly industrialized states generally possess a wider variety of pressure-groups and interests, and such groups and interests tend to possess more influence than is the case with traditional or developing states, with relatively small and simple governmental organizations. A comparison of the range of pressure-groups of the United Kingdom with those of Eire, the power of pressure-groups in the United States with those of Argentina, or in Italy compared to Egypt, illustrates this point.

CLOSED SYSTEMS

Closed political systems were defined above as systems organized on the assumption that it is desirable and possible to prevent influences from the domestic economic, social or cultural sub-systems of society, or from foreign political systems, from affecting political decisions. Such political systems may be theocracies (i.e. regimes controlled according to a set of religious values, by religious leaders or rulers who accept their powers as to be exercised according to the dictates of religion, such as medieval Catholic regimes), or totalitarian regimes of a leftist or rightist nature (e.g. the USSR, Communist China, Fascist Italy or Nazi Germany). The reason why they are closed in this fashion is because of a belief in political organizations as the proper interpreters and administrators of an ideology (usually a fairly explicit ideology in fact), and in politics as the primary activity in society, assimilating and controlling economic, social and cultural activity.

This has important consequences for the roles of parties and pressure-groups. Far from policies emerging as the result of their activities and influence within the political system, they are the vehicles for translating policies back to their membership and supporters. Usually there is only one party, which becomes almost identical in its top leadership to the leadership of the government, therefore the party accepts the goals set by its leadership (convert the heretics, harass the Jews, collectivize agriculture, denounce revisionists), and mobilizes first its own members, then the population as a whole, in support of these goals. However, parties do serve certain purposes in closed systems which they also serve in open systems, such as the discovery and training of recruits for leadership positions, political education and communication, and, in the pre-revolutionary period preceding the establishment of many of the closed systems, the formulation of ideology and the provision of means of competing against other groups for the power of the state.

Similarly, pressure-groups or interest-groups bear little relation to those in an open system. Since the 'party' or the 'state' or the 'Church' is the only interpreter of ideology, its policies are bound to be correct and therefore to try to change them, even by political persuasion and argument, is not only a waste of effort, but treasonable into the bargain. Two consequences of this should be noted. First, disagreement over policy, political strategy and values, and a competitive struggle for power do go on in a closed system, but *within* the party and political organizations, not *between* formally organized groups. Thus the 'anti-party' group in Soviet politics, the struggles between the SS and the SD in Hitler's regime, the various brands of Maoists in contemporary China, the 'old' and the 'new' Communists of Czechoslovakia, are all examples of such competition. Second, where organized groups do exist, they serve as party auxiliaries rather than as influences on the party or state. Thus trade unions in the USSR act as welfare agencies, channels of communication and overseers of the methods of management. The Nazis had their various organizations such as the Labour Front and ancillary sporting and cultural organizations, but all were seen as subservient to the party. Interests or loyalties beyond the control of the party are discouraged or even forbidden – religion, ethnic loyalties, the family itself. And for this purpose of making subservient all other aspects of social life to the political, censorship, legal restrictions, terror, ideology, education and any other available weapons are used.

THE OPEN SYSTEM

There is the greatest difference between presuming an opinion to be true. because, with every opportunity for contesting it, it has not been refuted, and assuming its truth for the purpose of not permitting its refutation. Complete liberty of contradicting and disproving our opinion is the very condition which justifies us in assuming its truth for purposes of action; and on no other terms can a being with human faculties have any rational assurance of being right.[2]

[2] J. S. Mill, *On Liberty*, 1859.

But it could not be less folly to abolish liberty, which is essential to political life, because it nourishes faction, than it would be to annihilate air, which is essential to animal life, because it imparts to fire its destructive agency.[3]

Whereas a closed political system finds its values and its goals in a prescribed ideology, be it Marxism, Christianity in its Protestant or Catholic forms, or the Aryan racism of Hitler, an open system claims no such single source of its values, but rather is prepared to allow individuals, groups, parties and classes to compete for the power to apply their ideas, values and policies through the institutions of the system. There is a value of the preservation of the system which is common to open and closed systems alike, but in an open system new ideas, arguments, even pressures of a self-interested kind are encouraged as beneficial to the political process, and, within broad limits, to the preservation of the system. In a closed system these are regarded as irrelevant at best, at worst a threat to the survival of the system itself.

The functions of political parties and pressure-groups in Britain have been discussed in earlier chapters.[4] It is worthwhile, though, to take a more general view of the functions of political groups in an open system, to understand better how in fact they do play a part in preserving the political system and assisting the workings of the political process.

The parties and pressure-groups in an open system supply information to those in authority. It is true that this function is also carried out by the party in a one-party state, but in such states as the USSR or Nazi Germany there are three serious limitations: the party is identified with the regime, and so any dissatisfaction, disagreement or other signs of stress may well be hidden from the party for as long as possible (one thinks of the 'July Plot' to kill Hitler, for example); even if party agents do find signs of stress, they may fail to appreciate their significance, because of their own commitment to the prevailing ideology; and, thirdly, even if they discover and appreciate such stress, fear of blame in a state which depends on terror may prevent them from passing on the information to the authorities. In an open system these limitations do not apply.

[3] *The Federalist*, No. IX.
[4] See Chapters 3 and 5 above.

People dissatisfied with the authorities can use opposition parties to express such dissatisfaction, and by-elections, local elections, press comment, opinion polls and similar indications of loss of support will either cause the authorities to change their policies, or at least will encourage them to counter-activity by defending their policies publicly (as with the US Democratic Party over Viet-Nam, or the British Labour Party over the prices and incomes policy). Opposition parties will be sensitive to such indications of governmental unpopularity, nor will they hesitate out of fear to amplify these criticisms, as this is the way they can win power at the next general election. Pressure-groups also supply information in this way, both of an objective type, by putting the case for or against a particular proposal of the government, and information regarding opinions and attitudes, for the support given to such pressure-groups will be to some extent a measure of approval or disapproval of the government's proposals.

Parties and pressure-groups in an open system are the means by which demands from the citizenry are focused and given political expression. Such a function is not really required in a closed system, for the authorities only accept the demands of the ideology as relevant to their considerations, and such demands are revealed through a process of theological or legal interpretation, not by the resultant of the conflicting opinions of the people. Thus the decision to re-nationalize the steel industry was taken because Labour had been elected in a majority in the House of Commons, and therefore had the power to put its policies into effect, but it did not claim that its right to do so was derived from carrying out the processes of history or the imperatives of some racial theory. On the other hand, the Papal Encyclical on birth control is announced as authoritative because it is in some way binding revelation of the laws of God, not because a majority of the Curia, or bishops, or the clergy or laity were in favour. The decision to change the law regarding abortion in Britain, though views on both sides were expressed in terms of values, including the 'laws of God', is accepted as an authoritative decision not because of its *content* but the process by which it was accepted by Parliament and promulgated.

Representation is a value in an open system which is not

found in closed systems, because it is not consistent with the notion of revealed truth found in closed systems. It may be objected that representation is a quality found in democracies, and that not all open systems are democracies. This is an important point, but an examination of oligarchies, benevolent despotisms, colonial rule as in the British and French empires before the Second World War, and even of 'open dictatorships' such as are possessed by certain contemporary South American states, shows that the notion of representation of interests, estates, classes, occupations, regions, and so forth may still be present in non-democratic regimes. Eighteenth-century England was not a democracy, yet a high value was placed on certain types of representation (even if such interpretation was uneven), and the quarrel with the American colonies was not over *whether* the colonies should be represented – the English Parliament claimed that they were already virtually represented – but *how*, and with what degree of importance relative to other interests. Several of the states of Latin America change from democratic to dictatorial rule from time to time, yet major interests within their social systems may still preserve their representation and their influence (the Catholic Church, commercial interests, the regions or provinces, etc.).

The essential distinction in political practice between the open and the closed system is just this – that in the open system interests from non-political sub-systems of society are permitted and encouraged to take part in the political process (e.g. by being granted seats in the legislature, or by being given formal opportunity to comment on pending legislation); organization, whether as competing parties or as interest-groups, is not illegal, and the authority of the decisions made in the name of the state derives from the representative nature of the institutions which have made them. It is not essential that every adult should have the vote in order that a political system be termed open or representative. In some states women do not have the vote (e.g. Switzerland), in others only literates, or members of certain classes, and so on. Yet the possibility of influencing the political process exists in such systems, as it did for the unfranchised working classes in nineteenth-century England, or for voteless native inhabitants of British colonies in the pre-war period, or even for persons under 21 in modern Britain, France or West Germany. All these persons could form or join groups, could put their case by various means, and could expect a hearing, even if their arguments were not always accepted in the end.

The most obvious example of such representation by parties or interest-groups is in the British legislative system. Political parties are the originators of much important legislation, sometimes adopting proposals put to them by pressure-groups, but more often deriving policy from their electoral platforms, the decisions of Conference, and the basic values of the party. However, when a Bill is in draft stage it is now the practice to seek out representatives of affected interests and to give them the opportunity to comment critically on the proposals. Such comments are not always heeded (indeed, they may be directly opposed to each other if they come from several groups), but when the Bill reaches the House it is not often that a Minister cannot say 'the Government has, of course, consulted with the relevant interests before introducing this legislation, and has taken note of their remarks'. Such a process is not only unlikely in closed systems such as Nazi Germany or Soviet Russia, but, because of the single source of truth which they have claimed, is unthinkable.[5]

DIVIDED SYSTEMS

In a number of states there exist political minorities who do not necessarily accept the authority of the existing state power over them as legitimate or proper. The recent events in Nigeria, where the Ibos attempted to form their own state of Biafra, the strength of separatist movements in Quebec, Scotland, Northern Ireland, Wales, parts of India, and even in Brittany and the Basque regions of Spain, the growth of Negro activist movements in the USA, all illustrate this point. To counter such divisive tendencies, various social and cultural mechanisms exist, such as education, the growth of cities, and industrialization, but political forces are of great importance also.

[5] It is true that the Stalinist Constitution of 1936 was preceded by a period of 'grass-roots' discussion, but (a) no non-party organizations existed to channel criticism, and (b) little notice was in any case taken of criticisms – the draft was almost unaltered when promulgated.

In some political systems, the Constitution itself will provide for certain integrative processes, for instance by having a federal second chamber of the legislature apportioned on a regional basis with the units equal (as with the US Senate), or almost equal (as with the West German Bundesrat), or by recognizing the right of the minority to a share of executive posts (as with the Turkish minority under the Cyprus constitution), or by official recognition of minority languages (as in Belgium, Switzerland or Canada). But one of the most important mechanisms of integration is the political party.

The party can serve an integrative function in three different ways. It can serve as a separate organ of influence or even power for a minority, as the Irish Nationalist Party did in the years before the 1922 settlement, or as the Arab parties do in Israel. A major party can allow a separate organization to serve a particular region, as the Christian Socialists do in Bavaria (they are the *de facto* Bavarian branch of the Christian Democrats, and the parties never oppose each other at an election), or to some extent as happens with British parties (the Unionists in the Conservative Party, and the Welsh and Scottish organizations of the Liberal Party). Or a party can attempt to contain a minority, give it a share, perhaps a disproportionate share, of office, patronage, and so forth, yet still act as a 'national' party. The Democrats up to 1952 served in this way to integrate the South with the rest of the United States, the Canadian Liberal Party pays considerable attention to Quebec in its distribution of party offices (and Cabinet seats when in power), while most western parties pay some attention to balance in terms of regional representation.[6]

In attempting to represent a regional or other minority, however, a political party may become the vehicle of disintegrative sentiment. The Irish Nationalists in the Westminster Parliament before the First World War may have postponed the break between Eire and the United Kingdom, by allowing the Irish a voice – at times, after the 1910 elections, for instance, a powerful voice – in the affairs of government, but it also permitted itself to be used, as a party, as a further weapon in the struggle for independence, by tactics of obstruction, for

[6] Where religion plays a part (as in West Germany, for instance) the question of balance is complicated still further.

example. The regional and tribal basis of Nigerian political parties did little to prevent the division of the country in 1967 when the Ibos felt that the new Nigerian regime was contrary to their interests.

The second and third solutions appear more likely to preserve integration in a state with potentially divisive tendencies. Certainly fears of Bavarian separatism in a West German state that was oriented very much towards the industrial (and ex-Prussian) North-West have diminished considerably with the continuous representation of the Christian Socialist Party in the German Government, and its indisputable influence on the majority party, the Christian Democrats. One measure of this is the decline in the popularity of the Bavarian Party, which won seventeen seats in the 1949 Bundestag elections, but has not won any since. The disinclination of the former Confederate states of the American South to form a separatist party has been at least partly due to its position within the Democratic Party, although this position is now weakening, with the waxing strength of the Republican Party in the southern states, and the identification of the Democrats with Negro aspirations, the power of the federal government and the problems of urban areas. And the recent victory of the Canadian Liberal Party – led by its new Quebeçois Leader, Pierre Trudeau – appears to have diminished separatist demands which had been given such prominence by de Gaulle's intervention during his 1967 visit.

The state, however, is not the only type of political system with which we need to be concerned. Earlier chapters have suggested that there may well be political disputes, and political methods of settling disputes, in political parties themselves, or in pressure-groups. This is also true of supra-national organizations, such as the United Nations, the European Economic Community, and the Communist bloc, and it is interesting to see what role parties and pressure-groups might play in these divided systems.

Formal parties do not exist in the United Nations Organization. Delegates represent their states, not the party in power at the time, in a similar way to Ambassadors. But groupings of delegates do exist, not on the basis of the party complexion of the government back home, but along a number of inter-related dimensions reflecting world political patterns. The free-world – neutralist – Communist division is the most obvious of such groupings, and this was to some extent encouraged by the *de facto* recognition by the founders and early delegates of a claim to balance by the Communist and non-Communist blocs. Thus, in a rather dubious deal to placate the Russians, the Western states agreed to support the admission of Byelorussia and the Ukraine, which gave Russia in effect three votes in the General Assembly. The Russian troika proposal, following the death of Dag Hammerskjöld, by which there would be a plural Secretary-Generalship, which would include one from each of the three blocs, was also a recognition of this division. An examination of voting patterns on matters affecting the cold war shows that there are regularities of voting on ideological lines, and informal tactical discussions among states likely to be on the same side take place before such debates, similar, in some respects, to party manœuvrings in the United States Senate. Another division within the United Nations is on the imperialist – colonial dimension, with the USA, France, the United Kingdom, the white Commonwealth countries, the Netherlands, Belgium and Portugal on the one hand, and the multitude of ex-colonies on the other. Here it is not unknown for the colonial states to classify the USSR as imperialist on certain issues, especially when its political interference becomes too blatant.

While there are obvious dangers in such hardening divisions within an organization like the United Nations, it is not an unmixed curse. It makes voting moderately predictable, it emphasizes to some of the newer and smaller states that they have allies who have similar problems and policies, it structures debate in the Assembly, and it may even, in time, lead to some kind of party government within the organization, which could be a means of regulating conflict just as party government in a national legislature may regulate domestic conflict.[7]

[7] It is important not to over-emphasize the discipline of the UN blocs. Andrew Boyd has called the pattern of voting in the General Assembly 'so complex that only a three-dimensional figure in rainbow colours could show it adequately' (*United Nations: Piety, Myth and Truth*, Penguin, 1964, p. 72). His general account of voting patterns is recommended to readers interested in the workings of the United Nations Organization (pp. 71–82).

While the basis of representation in the decision-making organs of the European Economic Community is the member-state, in the Parliament of the Community the political parties of the members take on considerable importance. Though the number of delegates appointed to the Community Parliament by their own parliaments is determined on a national basis (thirty-six each from France, West Germany and Italy, fourteen each from Belgium and Holland, six from Luxembourg), delegates in fact act as Socialists, Liberals and Christian Democrats, caucassing and voting, even holding the parliamentary offices, according to their political, not their national, sympathies. Should the proposed aim of the direct election of delegates to the European Parliament be achieved, this ready-made party basis would aid the electoral process, and would in turn be reinforced by it.

Interest-groups also have a formal role in the institutions of the Common Market, through the advisory Economic and Social Committee. Article 193 of the Treaty of Rome states:

There shall hereby be established an Economic and Social Committee with consultative status.

The Committee shall be composed of representatives of the various categories of economic and social life, in particular, representatives of producers, agriculturalists, transport operators, workers, merchants, artisans, the liberal professions and of the general interest.

Again allocation is by states, but under Article 195:

The Committee shall be composed in such a manner as to secure adequate representation of the different categories of economic and social life.

It also acts through specialized sections, such as those concerned with agriculture and transport.

The existence of parties and pressure-groups on a European basis has a tendency to moderate nationalist – and hence divisive – attitudes within the Common Market. They thus play an integrative role, and are available as parts of a future European political organization, should one develop. The German farmer, the French car-manufacturer, the Belgian transport operator, and the 'European' civil servant at work in Brussels, all represent 'European' interests, which must be taken into account by governments in their Common Market policies. And most of these interests are now, in one way or another, bound up with the continuation of the Common Market, though each may hope to benefit from development of the European Community in a different direction.

It is more and more apparent that, within the Communist political system, there are ideological divisions which affect the relations of the member-states. While the basic division is between the Russian group and China and her satellites, within these groups divisions may also be ascertained. Yugoslavia, Hungary and Poland were among the early rebels against Russian paternalist dictatorship, but the more subtle rebellion of Czechoslovakia has led to a new division, with the revisionist regimes of Yugoslavia and Roumania in support of the Czechs. Russia and East Germany, with Hungary and Poland in attendance, constitute the opposition to such liberalization policies. Many of the signs of party conflict of a primitive type can be observed: the quarrel over policies, the appeals for support, the declarations of legitimacy (and the illegitimacy of the opposition, at least on the part of Russian spokesmen), and the claims, also found in the Sino-Soviet quarrel, to be the 'true interpreter' of basic ideology, in terms of changing circumstances.

DEVELOPING SYSTEMS

One of the most significant phenomena of post-war political history is the multiplication of new independent states in the 'family of nations'. The main cause of this growth has been the ending of colonial rule within the former British, French, Dutch and Belgian empires. These new states, most of whom may generally be termed modernizing or developing in terms of their social, economic and political organizations, face several very serious problems more or less simultaneously, problems which each of the developed or industrialized states faced at various periods of their existence, over many decades, and generally not all at the same time. Among such problems are those of *nationalism*, the emotion that was instrumental in gaining independence, but which sections of the state may now use to challenge the new government with its own arguments of self-determination (as in Nigeria, India and the Congo); *authority*, for it is not as easy for a new government, lacking financial, military and human resources, to impose its will on every part of its territory as it was for an experienced imperial power; and *modernization*, in the economic sphere, which, even in a free enterprise economy, and more so in a populist-socialist regime, as chosen by many of the new states, requires above all a highly-skilled bureaucracy to administer the plans for development.

The role of political parties and pressure-groups in relation to these problems is often crucial. With regard to nationalism, for instance, as has been discussed above in relation to divided systems, political parties can serve as integrative mechanisms, focusing loyalties on nation-wide institutions in those cases where parties are not organized on the basis of region, religion, or tribe, and offering a sense of participation to its members and its supporters. Indeed, in many cases the prestige of the nationalist movement in gaining independence, often under a single charismatic leader, means that the nation possesses only one party, either naturally or by legal decree of the postcolonial government. Ghana under Nkrumah, Algeria under Ben Bella, Egypt under Nasser, and Tanzania under Nyerere are all examples of this. Similarly, where urbanization and industrialization have provided the necessary conditions for their development, interests such as trade unions, mercantile groups, religious and social organizations have also, by their activities and structure, provided national political institutions of a non-governmental type, through which the citizen can participate in his newly-independent political system. Despite coups, corruption, authoritarian organization and other features deplored by western observers brought up in a more democratic tradition, these organizations help to establish the identity of a new state at a time when (as with a growing child) a sense of identity is the prerequisite for further development.

Parties and pressure-groups contribute to the establishment of authority in new states by participating in the process of 'choosing' (even in non-democratic systems) a party leader to be head of state (as President or Prime Minister), and by taking part in policy-formation and the establishment of national goals. In states where independence came after a period of preparation, as with most of the former British colonies, the pre-colonial parties carried their organization and personnel over to provide the occupants of authority roles in the new states. In states where independence was wrested from the imperial power by conflict (as in Algeria) the nationalist revolutionary movement served the same purpose to some extent. Only where no such preparation took place (as in the Congo, and some Latin American states in the nineteenth century) was there a real crisis of authority.

The most valuable function of a party or pressure-group in a developing state is often the recruitment, training and employment of elites, who, as servants of the powers who form the government, can supplement or even act in place of a nonpolitical civil service. Even though developing states may lack widespread literacy among their inhabitants, the party activists must include personnel skilled in the arts of communication. Even though the state may lack organizers, the party, to be successful, both in an election and in holding on to power after an election, (and this applies even in a one-party state) must be able to call on organizational skills. As with Communist states, in many cases there is a considerable overlap of the state and party elites in developing nations. The experience of those who have received part of their education overseas has probably increased their political awareness at the same time as it has given them knowledge, so it is not surprising if these members of the elites of new states join political organizations. Especially if their skills can be employed in administration of development plans – in technology, the economic departments, public administration, the legal system, and so on – their value to the party, and the need to secure their loyalty to the party and its policies, become even more obvious.

Finally, parties and pressure-groups play an important role in defining goals for a developing state, and encouraging the population to work for those goals.

. . . The political parties of a modernizing society play an active entrepreneurial role in the formation of new ideas, in the establishment of a network of communication for those ideas, and in the linking of the public and the leadership in such a way that power is generated, mobilized, and directed.[8]

In a state whose population has been accustomed to the traditional routines of an agrarian economy, where the future was seen in cyclical terms of the repetition of routines rather than growth and development, where change is mistrusted and the familiar is welcomed for its familiarity, the significance of the party as an agent of change is hard to exaggerate. Whether in terms of social change (the spread of education, the elimination of certain diseases, provision of medical services, the creation of communications networks, reduction in the rate of population growth), economic change (investment plans, centralized marketing of crops, exploitation of mineral revenues, taxation policies, alteration in traditional work patterns), or political change (the encouragement of political participation, even in undemocratic regimes, the development of an able administrative service, negotiations for foreign aid, the creation of a 'national' politics rather then a regional or tribal politics, the possibility of alliances with other states), the party is paramount in supplying the plans, the organization and communications structure to make them known, and, in many cases, the personnel to carry them out.

The process is one of interaction, to a great degree. Modernization itself enables the political party to function more effectively by making it easier to obtain the resources it needs. It encourages economic and social specialization in the population (the USSR is a good example, with its multiple elites, even if they are not organized sufficiently or are not independent enough to be termed interest-groups), and such specialization encourages the creation of interest-groups. This pluralism in turn can provide the stimulus and the conflict out of which policies and programmes emerge on a national scale. W. W. Rostow has discussed the concept of 'economic take-off' – the level of investment which permits an increasing rate of economic growth to be maintained; it may be useful to look for a similar concept in political analysis, and indeed a certain degree of organization and activity of political parties and

[8] D. Apter, *The Politics of Modernization* (University of Chicago Press, 1965), p. 186.

pressure-groups would seem to be a necessary element in political modernization.

THE PLURAL SOCIETY

What are the implications of these comparative reviews of other systems for an understanding of British politics? First, western democracy, involving a fairly open political system, with political opinion, political influence and political values expressed through a galaxy of pressure-groups and an entrenched system of competitive parties, is not found in more than a handful of the 150 or so states that make up the independent countries of the world. There are many reasons for this. Such a system only comes about in certain economic and social conditions, involving, for example, fairly widespread education, a complex economy and a relatively high gross national product. It is probably not to be found in states lacking urban centres, as this would inhibit the growth – even the formation – of national organizations.

Second, there are no grounds for supposing that the Anglo-American forms of state, based on pluralism of political influence and organized parties competing for power, are in any way final or fully developed, nor that developing polities in Africa, Asia or Latin America will necessarily grow to imitate the Anglo-American models. If there is one thing certain in politics, it is that nothing is ever certain or final, and particularly in view of the built-in propensities for change in British society there is every reason to suppose that in fifty or one hundred years from now our political system, and the parties and pressure-groups that contribute so much to its operation, will be at least as different from their forms today, as the contemporary system is different from that of Gladstone or Peel. And it is already clear that several alternative models are available for developing nations to copy, even supposing that they wish to copy any at all: the closed Communist system, the federal model, the autocratic models (perhaps based on military rule, at least in the first instance), or even a Continent-wide model such as 'Europe' might become. As with technological development, so with political development: the latecomer is not compelled to follow the same path or make the same mistakes as the pioneer; he can jump ahead and adopt the latest designs.

Thirdly, it becomes more and more plain that, while certain aspects of political parties and pressure-groups may be found to be common to many states, either through imitation or simply because they are the common requirements of political systems (such as the need for leadership, or methods of obtaining finance), many other important features are unique since they reflect the formative influences of history and the culture and traditions of the country concerned. Where religion is a divisive force, this may be reflected in the institutional arrangements of the state (as in Lebanon), the political parties or the interest-groups. Where one region of a federation includes within its boundaries important economic resources, this may lead to parties based on these regions, and to the attempted break-up of the system (Nigeria, Katanga, the American South in the nineteenth century are examples). Even when the traditional divisions or the traditional foundations of political groups have lost their force over time, it is not easy to alter the fixed patterns that history has made. The major parties of West Germany, Socialists, Christian Democrats, Liberals, are survivors of Weimar and even Bismarckian ancestors, despite two world wars, inflation, depression, Nazi totalitarianism and the loss of half the territory of the original state. Farmers in an industrial state, veterans long after the wars they fought in are half-forgotten memories, feminists when the equality of the sexes has long been won – these and similar interest-groups not only maintain their existence, but sometimes much of their traditional influence as well. There is no rule which requires, in Britain or in any other state, that in the political system the balance of organized groups must accurately reflect the actual balance of important interests in the state, any more than parties reflect the actual contemporary division of the voters.

And so the final word in this chapter about the similarities and contrasts among parties and pressure-groups in various states must be to emphasize their diversity. This implies something else: the care that is needed in using the categories of party or pressure-group. Is there really anything in common among the British Conservative Party, the East German Socialist Unity Party, the Cuban or Chinese Communist

Groups and the political system: comparison and contrast 175

Parties, the Gaullists of France, the Kenya African National Union, and the Northern People's Congress that existed in the Nigerian Federation? Can the term pressure-group be applied to any purpose to groups as diverse as the Trades Union Congress in Britain, the sugar lobby in the United States, the Chinese in Malaysia, the Catholic Church in Spain, the military in Latin America, or student groups almost everywhere? Perhaps the answer is 'no'. Perhaps the categories are too broad. But, if care is taken to distinguish political groups not on the basis of what they call themselves (or are called by others) but according to what they do and how they are organized, then comparisons can reveal much.

9 Conclusion: the plural society

After this rather involved study of parties and pressure-groups in Britain, it is time to ask by way of summary: what has emerged? In the first place, it was suggested that a superficial view of the political process in a 'mass society' like Britain – densely populated, centralized in terms of economic, political and cultural institutions, with a small number of powerful communications media, each with a large public – might indicate an inevitable gap between government and governed, between 'them' and 'us', and would perhaps contrast unfavourably with a view of the past as a 'golden age' of political activity. But political parties, whose leaders occupy the offices of power, and numerous influential pressure-groups, who affect the policies of governments in various ways, do, by their existence, offer several opportunities for participation by citizens, ranging from voting, through group-membership, to office-holding within these organizations. And parties, by sharpening the focus of different views which people hold on various issues, help to make the political process more meaningful to the electorate.

The next three chapters dealt with aspects of political parties, and, in particular, with the two parties likely to have the opportunities (and the responsibility that goes with those opportunities) to form governments in the foreseeable future – Labour and the Conservatives. The rise of political parties in British politics was traced from the time of the Stuarts, but the crucial political and constitutional changes were those of the nineteenth and early twentieth centuries which, by enlarging the electorate, and simplifying and regulating the electoral process, made the modern type of nation-wide political party possible. The functions of parties were classified as obvious ones of winning elections in order to exercise political power, and developing sets of policies, and indirect or auxiliary functions such as political education and political socialization.

Examination of the organizational structures of the parties emphasized the differences between the parties, and revealed the three different 'levels' of organization which each possesses – the national, professional (or bureaucratic) and the parliamentary organizations. The post-war organizational changes of the parties, following, as they did so often, on electoral defeat, had quite considerable importance on their political behaviour. The question: 'What is it all for?' was answered by examining the manifestoes of the three parties represented in Parliament, since the presumption was made that these basic programmes are what each party wishes to use political power to achieve.

Parties are composed of people – the leaders and followers – and questions of how leaders are chosen, from what types of person, and why they seek leadership responsibilities are both interesting and important. Political experience, credibility, and certain leadership skills were emphasized as prerequisites for British party leadership. Since it is almost inevitable that the path to leadership runs through Parliament, and the House of Commons in particular, the selection process by which candidates commence political careers is especially interesting. Followers come in many shapes and sizes – and degrees of commitment. In particular, three types can be distinguished: the activist, who plays a key role in the local organization, and devotes much of his spare time to the party; the supporter, who does something positive for his party other than just voting for it; and the sympathizer, who regards his party as a team which he can support, and votes fairly regularly for it. The leader-follower relationship involves politics within parties, and this can have important consequences for the political system as a whole – as, for instance, when Sir Alec Douglas-Home was selected as Conservative Leader in 1963. Finance, which dictates so largely the extent to which a party can make an impact on the electorate, was also included as part of the section on party structure and organization.

Pressure-groups are more varied in purpose and organizational structure than political parties. Like parties, their political history extends chiefly from the industrial revolution and the extensions of the franchise in the nineteenth century. The recognition of the legitimacy of interests in the political process was an important trend, and one with considerable consequences for the British political system as it is today. Pressure-groups may be classified in various ways – by their permanent or temporary nature, their self-interested or altruistic purposes, their promotional or defensive strategies, and their general character: economic, social-cultural, or political. The targets of group action can be summarized as: public opinion, candidates and Members of Parliament, political parties, Parliament itself, and the executive departments of the government. Groups will follow a strategy of selecting targets which are consistent with *their* view of the power structure on a particular issue (even if, to an objective observer, such a view seems erroneous), always supposing that they have 'access' to such targets.

Pressure-groups, like parties, have their internal political problems, and have to exist in a system which may well contain other groups directly opposed to them, which they will have to take into account.

Groups in politics – parties and pressure-groups alike – are concerned with policy, and the idea of the ladder of values, i.e. the way in which a specific policy could generally be related to a more general set of principles, which in turn came from the application of basic values (or ideology) to some aspect of social life, seems to assist in an appreciation of this point. Not all social values can be attained through political means – but many of the more important and general ones can. The party manifestoes, and two legislative proposals, provided illustrations of the relationship between groups and policy. British parties, while fairly pragmatic in nature, none the less do possess an ideological base which is revealed from time to time, and certainly in this fashion they are differentiated from American parties.

Being value-oriented, how can parties represent or respond to the wishes of the electorate? The referendum has no place in British politics – nor is it likely to have. Pressure-groups and opinion-polls, as well as general, local and by-elections, play some part in conveying information on the state of public opinion to the parties. Pressure-groups also have problems over values. Much depends on how *specific* are the aims of the group, and on its organizational style.

Values motivate groups, but contrasting with such positive

factors are the negative limitations imposed by constraints of various kinds. By using the concept of the *system* to explain these constraints, they can be classified as coming from within the group, from within other parts of the political system, or from outside the system. Examples of such constraints include the scarcity of group resources, procedural limitations within the system, and demands from other sub-systems of society on social resources. But constraints can be turned into opportunities by skilled politicians.

In order to achieve a more sensitive appreciation of the important aspects of political groups in British society, the next chapter undertook a brief comparative survey of the functions of political groups in other societies, classed as open, closed, divided and developing systems. In turn, the structure of such systems was seen to have effects on the behaviour of groups.

And so the discussion returns to the British context, and in particular to the questions: what are the consequences of the existing system of political groups, and their values and behaviour, for the British polity (or political system)? and what are the consequences for British society?

THE CONSEQUENCES FOR THE POLITY

Several sections of this book have offered evidence to show that the British political system is – in the phrase employed in the last chapter – an open system, and this can, by extension, also be called a plural system. A plural system is one in which, first, no exclusive source of basic values or political principles is recognized; rather, such values, principles, ideals and ideas come from many different sources, such as parties, pressure-groups, the Civil Service, local government bodies, media of public communication, economic, cultural and religious organizations, and so on. Second, it involves a reliance on the political process to provide acceptable (not imposed) solutions or compromises through the competition of these different institutions and groups. This competition is chiefly that between political parties, for they will often include within their policy programmes the more significant demands of pressure-groups. But pressure-groups and interests – whether economic, cultural, charitable, religious, political, ethnic, or what have you – are free to use the various channels of influence open to them.

Nor is this idea of a plural political system new. It can be traced back at least to 1688,[1] possibly to the Reformation. The British political tradition is a tradition of participation, even though the politically effective population was, until the late nineteenth century, only a small proportion of the whole. The oligarchic parties of pre-1868 did not ignore the public out-of-doors, nor did they assert that the unfranchised classes had no claim to their consideration. Within limits (and there was often disagreement about these limits being too narrowly circumscribed) the working-class, women, aliens, and other interests not represented directly through the franchise, could seek to influence the political process quite legitimately by petitioning, pamphlets, demonstrations, meeting with politicians, and so on. Along with this tradition of participation is a strong belief in the legitimacy and efficacy of political solutions – of 'ballots, not bullets'. One report pointed out that in Great Britain:

> The participant role is highly developed. Exposure to politics, interest, involvement, and a sense of competence are relatively high. There are norms supporting political activity, as well as emotional involvement in elections . . . there is general system pride as well as satisfaction with specific governmental performance.[2]

If other chapters have stressed the effects of these features of the British political system on parties and pressure-groups, it is necessary here to emphasize the effects that vigorous, open, nationally-organized groups have on maintaining these features. Knowledge about politics, interest in politics, the sense of participation in politics, the belief in the legitimacy of political solutions – these all depend to a substantial degree on the existence, and the vigorous development, of political groups. The diffuse demands of a scattered and otherwise politically unorganized public are focused by these groups into sharper issues, capable of debate and settlement (e.g. on Sunday observance, policy for higher education, spending on defence,

[1] The various interests involved in the substitution of Prince William of Orange for James II on the British throne are an indication of the notion of 'plurality' at the time.
[2] G. Almond and S. Verba, *The Civic Culture* (Princeton, 1963), p. 455.

road safety measures). They seize on problems of our society – and the competitive political process encourages the parties and pressure-groups to seize on them – in an attempt to ameliorate them through the agency of political institutions. Thus Oxfam and Christian Aid appeal for charitable contributions to aid the poor in underdeveloped countries; large corporations may find it financially attractive to invest in economic development schemes for such countries; social and cultural contacts with British organizations may help in various ways. But potentially the most effective solutions to problems of overseas development (if the solutions are within the power of *any* elements of British society) can be provided through Parliament and the government, prodded and persuaded by political parties and pressure-groups.

There is a danger – pointed out from time to time particularly by left-wing Labourites or right-wing Conservatives – that in the day-to-day political world, the British method of stressing empirical solutions to problems carries with it the danger in the longer-term of over-emphasizing consensus, and avoiding conflict, especially conflict of principles or values (as distinct from conflict of methods). The term 'Butskellism' was coined to sum this up in a slightly sarcastic fashion. *Tribune*, Nye Bevan and Michael Foot, Enoch Powell, Duncan Sandys and the Monday Club have all prophesied the dangers that might arise from reliance on consensus politics. There *is* a danger, for the tyranny of a single-party state, or a single received opinion or conventional wisdom may be no less a tyranny for being reached by majority vote. In particular, unorganized or unrepresented interests (briefly considered in Chapter 5 above) may suffer by any such trend.

There are various forces working within the social and political systems which make for consensus, such as education, the mass media, the system of social security, a high standard of living. The policy process, both pre-legislative and post-legislative, places a high value on agreement – agreement with affected interests, agreement (if possible) between at least the frontbench elements of the major parties, agreement between legislative and executive, between central and local authorities, and so on. One might say that the more potentially divisive the issue is, the greater the pressures for consensus become. The colour question in the 1964 and 1966 general elections, with a number of local exceptions, was played down by tacit agreement among the three major parties. House of Lords reform has always, where possible, been dealt with by an all-party committee, and, indeed, if this committee has failed to agree, unilateral action by the majority party has generally been inhibited.[3] The recent Speaker's Conference on electoral reform is another all-party committee of a 'constitutional' nature. Rightly or wrongly, the war policies of the Churchill National Government of 1940–5 were rarely, if ever, subjected to organized party criticism. Though often only a disguised plea that their own point-of-view should prevail, the demands by politicians and others that certain divisive issues be 'taken out of politics' or 'settled once and for all' also reflect the value placed on consensus. Returning to the example of the re-nationalization of steel, for instance, this view was expressed quite frequently, and by MPs of all parties: 'Let us keep the subject out of the field of controversy. . . . ' (Sir R. Nugent, col. 1616)[4]; 'People are heartily fed up with seeing steel knocked backwards and forwards like a shuttlecock over the political net. . . . ' (E. Hooson, col. 1661); 'Throughout the years the House of Commons and the Governments of the day have been able to secure the public acceptance of their Measures only when they have had the general consensus of national opinion behind them on major issues of this nature.' (D. Donnelly, col. 1672). A similar view is often taken of religious, educational, penal and constitutional matters.

Now it is plain, as Desmond Donnelly claimed, that, especially in a democratic or plural political system, the government must not only govern, but govern legitimately. This means that it must be able to claim popular support for its measures, or at least for the principles on which they are based. Electoral victory is enough, for a time, to substantiate this claim, *for issues foreshadowed in the party manifesto* and for actions taken in response to the day-to-day demands imposed by domestic and international events. But, as the electoral victory passes

[3] The abandonment, as a result of its lengthy early consideration in the Commons, of the Wilson Government's Lords Reform Bill (1969) is further persuasive evidence of this.

[4] These quotations are from Hansard (HC *Debates*, (711), 6 May 1965).

further and further into history, other signs of support or opposition are heeded – public opinion polls, by-election results, press comment, even demonstrations. And it can be asserted that new policies, not foreshadowed in the election campaign, are not possessed of this legitimacy unless some degree of consensus can be obtained. It is vital to appreciate the distinction between 'ought' and 'is' here. Legally, constitutionally, politically, a party with a parliamentary majority – even if only a single-figure majority – can pass what legislation it will, subject only to the constraints of procedure, time, and the continued support of its back-benchers. Morally, ethically, one can question the legitimacy of such legislation in terms of the support it possesses. Objectively, it is even possible to devise measures of such legitimacy in terms of, for instance, opinion polls, observation of the law, and other responses of the public.

Recent works which have dealt with British politics in terms of its parties and pressure-groups, and recent political practice which has laid such stress on obtaining a consensus between, say, unions and employers on economic policy, or teachers and administrators on education policy, have tended to overlook the third party to such a consensus – the public. It is true that there is now no lack of information about public opinion, especially through the use of polls and surveys of various kinds, but the attitude of those presenting such surveys shows that the results are regarded as a kind of 'audience effect' – applause or annoyance after the action has occurred, rather than proper influence on the action itself. So it is perhaps worthwhile making two assertions about political groups and consensus, and looking briefly at some of the implications.

(i) *While consensus is a necessary element in legitimate government, it is important that such consensus takes account of interests of the unorganized 'general public', as well as the organized interests concerned in a particular policy.*

(ii) *Consensus is not a sufficient element to ensure democratic government; conflict has an important role also, and it is a function of political parties, and of other groups which concern themselves in politics from time to time, to focus opposing opinions on political issues.*

If, on the basis of earlier chapters and the earlier argument of this chapter, these assertions are accepted as valid, then several implications for the political system follow.

First, there is the need for more information, more publicity and more education about the British political process and specific parts of it, such as the making of policy and its execution. This would have several effects; it would increase the sense of public participation, it would be a salutary check on careless bureaucratic action (as the creation of the Parliamentary Commissioner will be, at least as suggested by the experience of other countries which possess some type of Ombudsman), and it would compel politicians to justify their decisions much more to the public, as well as to their consciences, party whips and interest-groups, just as the reasoned decisions of judges take account of the parties in the case *and* the public, even in civil cases. While the education system, mass media and the government itself (perhaps borrowing from the more savoury features of the West German Press and Information Office) could play an important role in this process, so, too, can parties and pressure-groups. The parties especially, by regarding the public as actors in the political system and not just a kind of voting audience, could help by widening the distribution of the very effective policy background pamphlets which they provide for party members, candidates, etc., by providing forums for civic discussion, especially on matters of local interest (planning decisions, comprehensive education, immigration, housing policies, the local authority budgetary process, transport policies), and by various other methods of communication with the public which are too often confined to the month or so before an election. Pressure-groups similarly could pay more attention to the way they present their case, and could also be encouraged to regard the public as a party to any bargain they seek to extract from the government, be it a decision on pit closures favouring the Mineworker's Union, a concession on investment grants for industrialists, an increase in certain agricultural price support levels, the delay or defeat of a Bill removing restrictions on Sabbath activities, or the choice of location of a new airport.

Secondly, it must be appreciated by the parties and the public that there is an obvious conflict between the governing and the policy formation functions of political parties, and that this calls, if not for revolutionary changes in party structure, at least for an adjustment of attitudes within the leadership echelons of the parties. It is this conflict which leads to the situation of the Prime Minister and the Cabinet giving priority to immediate reactions to circumstances (such as the balance of payments) in accordance with their governing function, and in doing so coming into conflict with the stated values of the majority party; these can still be pleaded forcefully by backbenchers, lacking the responsibility of office – and the result may be the decline in party morale, the failure of communications so often seen even in parties with large majorities. It can affect the opposition also, by placing their leadership in a position of having to seem a responsible alternative government, while others in the party are clamouring for aggressive opposition to everything the governing party is doing. The solution? There may not be any simple answer, but if this conflict of objectives were clarified, within the parliamentary parties especially, and if greater allowance were made for 'rebels' who put the values of the party first, so that they did not risk expulsion from the party or the downfall of the Government,[5] the interests of the party, of Parliament, and of the public might be better served.

Thirdly, in a two-party system which is as well established as it is in Britain, there might be a critical role for third parties as permanent opposition or ideas organizations, with the task of challenging the consensus in the name of minorities, unrepresented and unorganized interests, or simply in the name of an enlightened public interest – though it is readily admitted that appeal to this concept could be dangerous and could be open to many types of abuse. The Liberal Party, in the post-war years, has been more a source of critical challenge to the orthodoxies of the two main parties, and an originator of exciting policy ideas (entry into Europe, co-partnership schemes in industry, elected regional authorities, and so forth) than a challenge to the *power* of Labour or the Conservatives. It could well adopt this role more directly, if it were content to do so, and ready to decide on electoral tactics designed to consolidate

[5] The adoption of a 'constructive' vote of no confidence – a separate vote on whether or not the government should continue in power following on defeat on a substantive matter – would be a possible remedy.

its representation in Parliament and on local councils. Non-party groups might also develop in this way – some kind of political Consumers' Association, able to employ or hire the talents of lawyers, economists, business consultants, social scientists, accountants, planners, in order to challenge proposed or extant policies in the name of efficiency, value for money for the tax-payer, legality, conformity with broad social values (to the extent that these can be ascertained) – might meet the need, in the way that the National Council for Civil Liberties already tries directly to so do in one area of policy.

These ideas are perhaps not sufficiently coherent to be adopted immediately, nor are they, of course, the only possible methods of improving the functioning and responsiveness of the political system; obviously other aspects of political change – such as reform of Parliament and the Civil Service – are vital also. But change there surely must be; even in Britain it is not impossible for a system of centuries to be warped or toppled by any one, or a combination, of several occurences: military defeat, economic depression, an increase in political disturbances from the anarchic Left, the extreme Right, or an impatient 'central' group of radicals, or, locally, by nationalist groups (as has happened already in Ulster), social tensions – in areas of high immigrant densities, for instance – or developments in other states, especially the USA, West Germany or France. A political system that is to retain its flexibility, its responsiveness to social change, must be capable of adapting itself.

THE CONSEQUENCES FOR SOCIETY

. . . The formal power of British government cannot be used instantly to make or prevent changes in the natural social order outside the broad limits set by the structure of that order and its development, in which the longer-term effect of government action is only one of the factors. Great Britain is, socially and politically, a pluralistic society, in which the government no more than any other group or institution is outside the interaction of social forces that constitute the society. British politics is by nature the politics of compromise.[6]

[6] A. Potter, in R.Dahl (ed.), *Political Oppositions in Western Democracies* (Yale University Press, 1966), p. 33.

In so far as they are part of the political system, with functions relating to the distribution of decision-making powers in British politics, parties and pressure-groups have been considered as having consequences for the polity. The consequences for society arise from the fact that they are also social organizations, with some functions that are not to be regarded as only political, and from the wider implications of aspects of their political functions for the social system as a whole. (The term social system is used to include the political, social-cultural, legal, economic and other sub-systems of society as a whole.)

For example, in law, pressure-groups and political parties are almost entirely regarded as private institutions, free to develop rules and practices, free to organize, free to conduct their affairs, in the same way as, say, a manufacturing concern, an amateur dramatic society or a religious sect. Of course, they must have regard for the general constraints of the law: they must comply with taxation regulations, they must conduct their affairs with other groups or persons according to the laws of contract or tort (saving the special statutory provisions for trade unions), and, if they wish to register as friendly societies or charities, they must comply with the prescribed requirements. But that is all. There is no aspect of constitutional law that treats them yet as part of the political process (as mentioned on page 59, the parties are not yet even allowed to be mentioned on nomination or ballot papers in the electoral process, for instance). No legal requirements cover their internal political procedures – so the very props on which our pluralistic democracy rests need not themselves qualify as democratic. No legal requirements govern their internal judicial procedures – so the very groups which may criticize government policy for not observing the 'rule of law' or the 'natural rights' of, say, women, motorists, immigrants or trade unionists, may themselves be paying scant regard to either principle by expelling members without proper judicial safeguards, punishing them without trial, or settling disputes or controlling the powers of their executive without judicial procedure. No law yet exists which emulates the American requirement of registration of lobbyists and declaration of the sources of their funds, though it may be imagined that the democratic political process would require such disclosure in

Britain, especially from representatives of foreign interests, as may be the case with the recent Arab, Biafran, East German or Greek lobbies.

Yet these groups, as this book has sought to demonstrate, have public obligations, and in consequence there is a case to be made for at least some degree of public regulation of their organization and structure.[7] The government of the day is – and is likely to continue to be – a *'party'* government, the Prime Minister with his ever-expanding personal powers a *party* Leader. Few restrictions exist on party membership, but are the powers of that membership in electing officers, in selecting candidates (who, as Members of Parliament, elect the Leader), and in influencing policy safeguarded through the democratic process? Important groups possess considerable influence over the making and execution of policy decisions in their areas of interest, sometimes with legal sanctions for their advisory role laid down in an Act of Parliament. Yet they may be unrepresentative of their membership, they may have leaders selected under suspicious circumstances (the notorious ETU case was only a few years ago, in which the courts had to decide on certain matters regarding the elections in that union[8]), and they may freely expel opponents from membership in order to stifle criticism of particular policies. There is now a public interest involved in parties and pressure-groups, and it is time that Parliament agreed on certain basic uniform regulations by which these groups should conduct their affairs.

The existence of a two-party system, and of a wide range of varied interest-groups, as the main channels of communication of demands from the public (both as individuals and as members of various organizations in society) affects society in a number of other ways. Broad political loyalties, deriving from

[7] The 'Basic Law' of the Federal German Republic requires (Article 21) political parties to have internal organization which conforms to democratic principles. They must also publicly account for the sources of their funds.

[8] This case arose over allegations by members of the Electrical Trades Union that the 1959 election for the post of General Secretary had been 'rigged', in order to ensure the election of the Communist candidate. The court upheld this allegation in 1961, and the defeated candidate was declared elected. The union was disaffiliated from both the TUC and the Labour Party, but was later readmitted after its rules had been revised to ensure fair electoral procedures in the future.

parental attitudes, residential, educational and occupational environments and various other sources, are among the most important and the most widespread marks of social identity. Where once religion, or occupation, or locality served as the primary loyalties outside the family, these have been now often replaced with indication of political preference. How many of the characters of Dickens, for example, were given political alignments in the author's description? Yet today such preferences are frequently indicated in modern novels, even of a non-political setting. Further indications of the widespread nature of political alignment are given by the statistics on voting, for instance (more people vote than attend church) or the number prepared to express political preferences in the opinion polls (the 'don't know' replies range from about 10 per cent–30 per cent, though, if pressed, many of these will commit themselves to some clear choice). Newspapers are most obviously classified first on a serious-popular basis, but next on their left-wing – right-wing tendency. Even persons who do not regard themselves as in any sense politically committed (in party terms) may well have strong views on a particular policy-issue that affects their interests – incomes policy, the drink-and-drive legislation, immigration, comprehensive education. And though the schismatic quarrels of the post-Reformation period, or the divisions of the days of the Civil War, no longer separate members of the family one from another on matters of religion, or of constitutional rights, the arguments of the Garnetts on television owed much of their entertainment value to their familiarity, their similarity to real-life situations which many of us must have come across at some time or another in the home, the pub, the Armed Forces, or the works canteen.

Other examples spring to mind, that could be discussed at some length. The churches are affected, both by the greater care that they must take to avoid party politics when it is so pervasive a force and divisive an issue among church-attenders, and their need, if they are to secure benefits for themselves as organizations, to take part as interests in the political process. Economic organizations have to decide whether a partisan or a bi-partisan attitude to the parties is likely to have the consequences most favourable to their interests. This is especially important now that financial support must be disclosed in the company accounts of corporations. The jungle of social services and other bureaucratic areas of everyday life is often best explored with the aid of an intermediary, and the local councillor or Member of Parliament is one of the most obvious of such intermediaries now. Representation on consumer or advisory councils dealing with everything from the postal services and the supply of gas to the control of the police and the local hospitals is generally based on party balance. Politics, in a plural society, includes everything and pervades everything.

THE LAST WORD: DEMOCRACY?

... How is the word 'democracy' to be interpreted? My idea of it is that the plain, humble, common man, just the ordinary man who keeps a wife and family, and goes off to fight for his country when it is in trouble, goes to the poll at the appropriate time, and puts his cross on the ballot-paper showing the candidate he wishes to be elected to Parliament – that he is the foundation of democracy. And it is also essential to this foundation that this man or woman should do this without fear, and without any form of intimidation or victimization. He marks his ballot-paper in strict secrecy, and then elected representatives meet together and decide what government, or even, in times of stress, what form of government, they wish to have in their country. If that is democracy, I salute it. I espouse it. ... Democracy is not based on violence or terrorism, but on reason, on fair play, on freedom, on respecting the rights of other people.[9]

Finally, it is at last necessary to consider the question: can the plural society which Britain has become, with its paraphernalia of political parties and interests and pressure-groups, be called a democracy? If so, how do parties and pressure-groups relate to the preservation of a democratic society?

There are many definitions of 'democracy', and they range so widely that not all of them overlap. In other words, there is no central core to the definition, whether one appeals to history (via the Greek, Roman, Swiss and New England models), or to

[9] Extracts from a speech by Winston Churchill in the House of Commons, 8 December 1944, quoted in his history of the Second World War, volume VI, *Triumph and Tragedy* (Reprint Society edition, 1956), p. 245.

a constructed classification on the lines of the Platonic or Aristotelian typologies, or to some kind of common usage. However, many people would agree that a democracy would involve the presence of some or all of the following elements:

- The participation of the whole citizenry in the political process, on a more or less equal basis, if necessary via the election of representatives;
- the ability of the citizenry to affect the choice of leadership and to bring about changes in the leadership by institutional means (generally by the election process);
- the opportunity for the citizenry to influence policy decisions, and, conversely, the responsibility of the government to attend to such influence;
- the ready availability and diffusion of information about policies and the political process in order that citizens can make informed political choices;
- entrenched safeguards (usually including 'the rule of law') for minority rights.

It would seem that Britain, through its pattern of political institutions, and the diffusion of power among them, qualifies in these terms, though in some respects more than in others.

Political parties and pressure-groups perform many functions which help to carry out these requirements of democracy. They enable the citizenry to participate through the support – even the membership – of a party or organized group; they provide representatives and leaders, responsive to public opinion in formulating policies; they help to transmit information concerning political matters; they are often foremost in the defence of minority rights.

This is not to say that other methods of filling these requirements could not be found, but it is legitimate to claim that the present system of parties and groups, operating in a climate of opinion that accepts, and indeed often places reliance on, their participation in the political process, is fairly effective. Yet their existence is not an unmixed blessing. Especially under our unwritten (and therefore so very flexible) constitution, parties and groups may become undemocratic in themselves, and may embrace policies and values dangerous to democracy. They may, if successful in elections, change by law the legal framework and the institutions on which democracy depends. There are no entrenched provisions as in the West German or United States constitutions, nor any system of judicial review of breaches of the constitution through the legislative process under the British system of parliamentary sovereignty. The example of Hitler's attainment of the dictatorial powers he wielded is instructive. He came to office, and his party came to power, through what was, at least on the surface, a constitutional process. Yet he could then, quite legally, pass an 'Enabling Act' that abolished all parties other than his own, and consolidated his powers into a dictatorship of the severest kind. Many of the satellite states of Eastern Europe and of the one-party dictatorships of the newer states of Africa and Asia, observed every requirement of the law, yet became dictatorships for all that. In an age of mass communications, of technological developments, of a distrust of 'normal' politics, the party and the organized interest-group may be sources of danger to democracy.

If trust in the processes of the law, the institutions of society, and the organization of parties and pressure-groups is not enough to safeguard democracy, what is? Not to abandon these, certainly not, Goldwater-fashion, to turn to a vision of a simpler, less complicated and less politically demanding past, not to decry ineffectually the inexorable march of time and the changes it brings. The answer, if answer there be, is to work within and through existing institutions, to encourage people to value them and the system they are part of, to distrust the simple solutions in politics, and to be patient with the complicated processes of politics itself.

The real way of protecting democracy against the toxins that it secretes within itself in the course of its development does not lie in cutting it off from modern techniques for organizing the masses and recruiting leaders – such an operation would make of it an empty vessel, a vain show – but in diverting these to its use, for they are in the last resort mere tools, capable no doubt of being used for good as well as for evil. To refuse to use them is to refuse to act. If it were true that democracy were incompatible with them, this would no doubt mean that democracy is incompatible with the conditions of the present day. All the speeches upon the benefits of craftsmanship and the evils of industrialization do not alter the fact that the artisan's day is done and that we live in an age of mass production; regrets for the individualist and decentralized cadre parties of the nineteenth century and imprecations against the vast centralized and disciplined parties of today do not alter the fact that the latter alone suit the structure of contemporary societies.[10]

[10] M.Duverger, *Political Parties* (Methuen, 2nd edition, 1959), p. 427

Further reading

For readers interested in pursuing further some of the themes of this book, the following selection of books may be helpful. They do not constitute either a comprehensive or a critical bibliography on the topic of parties and pressure-groups in Britain. In some of the books, more comprehensive bibliographies will be found anyway.

THE HISTORY AND ORGANIZATION OF POLITICAL PARTIES

F. Bealey, J. Blondel and W. McCann, *Constituency Politics*, (Faber, 1965)
A. J. Beattie (ed.), *British Political Parties*, (2 vols, Weidenfeld & Nicolson, 1970)
Ivor Bulmer-Thomas, *The Growth of the British Party System*, (2 vols, John Baker, 1965)
Sir Ivor Jennings, *Party Politics*, (3 vols, Cambridge University Press, 1960-2)
R. T. McKenzie, *British Political Parties*, (Heinemann, 2nd edn. 1964)
Henry Pelling, *A Short History of the Labour Party*, (Macmillan, 1961)
Jorgen Scott Rasmussen, *The Liberal Party*, (Constable, 1965)
Alan Watkins, *The Liberal Dilemma*, (MacGibbon & Kee, 1966)
Trevor Wilson, *The Downfall of the Liberal Party*, (Collins, 1966)

LEADERS AND FOLLOWERS

Jean Blondel, *Voters, Parties and Leaders*, (Penguin, 1963)
Lewis Broad, *The Path to Power*, (Muller, 1965). (Brief biographies of the political careers of the men who became Prime Minister in the twentieth century)
W. L. Guttsman, *The British Political Elite*, (MacGibbon & Kee, 1965)
Anthony Howard and Richard West, *The Making of the Prime Minister*, (Jonathan Cape, 1965). (Inside story of the events

leading to the selection of Harold Wilson as Labour Party Leader, and his success at the 1964 general election)
Robert McKenzie and Allan Silver, *Angels in Marble: working class Conservatives in urban England*, (Heinemann, 1968)
Eric A. Nordlinger, *The Working Class Tories*, (MacGibbon & Kee, 1967)
Austin Ranney, *Pathways to Parliament*, (Macmillan, 1965)

PRESSURE-GROUPS

James B. Christoph, *Capital Punishment and British Politics*, (Allen & Unwin, 1962). (Deals with the political campaigns for the abolition of capital punishment)
Harry Eckstein, *Pressure-Group Politics*, (Allen & Unwin, 1960). (A study of the British Medical Association in its political role, especially concerning the National Health Service policies of the Attlee Government)
S. E. Finer, *Anonymous Empire*, (Pall Mall, 1958). (A concise treatment of the range and activities of pressure-groups and lobbies in British politics)
Roger Fulford, *Votes for Women*, (Faber, 1957). (The political struggles to obtain the enfranchisement of women)
Martin Harrison, *Trade Unions and the Labour Party since 1945*, (Allen & Unwin, 1960)
Allen Potter, *Organized Groups in British National Politics*, (Faber, 1961)
J. D. Stewart, *British Pressure Groups*, (Oxford University Press, 1958). (The activities of pressure-groups with special reference to their parliamentary strategies)
H. H. Wilson, *Pressure Group: the Campaign for Commercial Television*, (Secker & Warburg, 1961)
Graham Wootton, *The Politics of Influence*, (Routledge & Kegan Paul, 1963). (A study of the politics of British ex-servicemen's organizations, 1917–57)

ELECTIONS, POLITICAL COMMUNICATION AND THE MAKING OF POLICY

J. G. Blumler and D. McQuail, *Television in Politics*, (Faber, 1968)

D. E. Butler and Anthony King, *The British General Election of 1966,* (Macmillan, 1966)
R. L. Leonard, *Elections in Britain,* (Van Nostrand, 1968)
P. G. J. Pulzer, *Political Representation and Elections in Britain,* (Allen & Unwin, 1967)
Richard Rose, *Influencing Voters,* (Faber, 1967)
Colin Seymour-Ure, *The Press, Politics and the Public,* (Methuen, 1968)

BRITAIN: THE 'PLURAL SOCIETY'

Samuel H. Beer, *Modern British Politics,* (Faber, 1965)
Richard Rose, *Politics in England,* (Faber, 1965)
Anthony Sampson, *Anatomy of Britain Today,* (Hodder & Stoughton, 1965)

In addition there are several biographies of party leaders which chronicle the various historical and organizational crises of the British political scene over the past half-century.

Index

Attlee, C. R., 11 n., 27, 52, 53, 56–7

Baldwin, Stanley, 3. 27
Bevan, Aneurin, 50, 52, 66, 120, 151, 181
Brown, George, 34, 55–6, 62, 70, 115
Burke, Edmund: definition of party, 17; speech to electors of Bristol, 58
Butler, R. A., 40, 50, 74
By-elections, 3, 66, 183 (for individual constituencies, see under Constituencies)

Cabinet: and policy, 32, 185; and pressure-group activity, 103–5; social characteristics, 62
Callaghan, James, 62, 70
Campaign for Democratic Socialism, 9
Campaign for Nuclear Disarmament, 79, 90, 91, 97–8, 105, 127, 128, 136, 145
Castle, Barbara, 62, 120
Catholic Church: in medieval Europe, 9, 159; in Italian politics, 148; political parties and, 9; pressure-group activity, 92, 131, 163
Churchill, Winston, 11, 27, 52, 74, 182, 190 n.
Civil Service: and group activity, 103–5
Coalitions, 30, 144
Commercial television, 32, 94, 102, 106

Common Market, the (EEC), 2, 31, 34, 46, 47, 70, 90, 97, 106, 113, 121, 123, 132, 166, 168–9
Communications media, 5, 25, 82, 104–5, 137–8, 142–3, 150, 181, 192
Communist Party, 8, 138, 144, 146
Confederation of British Industry, 80, 81, 91, 99, 106, 136
Conservative Party: and pressure-groups, 99; candidate selection, 65; Central Council, 41; Chairman of Party, 43, 138; Conference, 41; distribution of power, 73–4; finance, 75–6; headquarters, 43; housing target at 1950 Conference, 31; ideology of, 110–14, 129; method of electing Leader, 28, 69–71; National Union of Conservative Associations, 22; 1922 Committee, 32, 38; 1966 manifesto, 47–8,112–13; organization, 37, 43; policies, 60, 139; post-1945 reforms, 27, 43, 45; Resale Price Maintenance Act and, 113–14, 115, 121–2; Selwyn Lloyd Report on Party Organization, 43
Constituencies: Bexley, 56; Bournemouth East and Christchurch, 66; Brighton Kemptown, 2, 3; Carmarthen, 2; Colne Valley, 3; Coventry South, 64; Dorset South, 8;

Constituencies–*cont.*
East Fulham, 3; Hamilton, 66; King's Lynn, 3; Leyton, 66; Liverpool Exchange, 64; North Devon, 56; Orpington, 3, 66; Peterborough, 2; St George's, Westminster, 3; Smethwick, 98; Twickenham, 8, 98; Wednesbury, 66; Wellingborough, 3
Co-operative movement, 99

Davies, E. Clement, 52, 72
Democracy, 6–7, 10, 35, 46, 64, 77, 86, 129, 132, 151, 163, 173, 182, 183, 187, 190–3
Donnelly, Desmond, 55, 66, 115–16, 120, 182
Douglas Home, Sir Alec, 11 n., 28, 34, 40, 52, 53, 55, 56, 62, 69, 70–1, 177

Eden, Anthony, 34, 52, 56
Election broadcasts, 3
Electoral reform, 47, 147, 182
Electoral registration, 19
Electoral system, 156
European Economic Community (EEC), (*see* Common Market)
Exclusion Crisis (1679), 14

Female suffrage, 26, 97, 127
Foot, Michael, 55, 117, 120, 181
France, 87, 90, 125, 129, 138, 144, 146, 150, 154, 155, 156, 158, 163, 164, 167, 168, 169, 175, 186
Fulton Committee on the Civil Service, 80, 143–4
Functional Representation, 61

Gaitskell, Hugh, 31, 52, 70, 110, 115

General election: 1832, 4; 1900, 24; 1906, 24; 1931, 27; 1950, 30; 1951, 30; 1959, 38, 45; 1964, 3, 30, 38, 64, 182; 1966, 2, 38, 46, 64, 182
General Strike (1926), 87, 127
Germany, 9, 40, 58, 87, 90, 115, 122, 129, 152, 154, 155, 156, 157, 158, 160, 164, 165, 166, 168, 174, 184, 186, 188 n., 192
Government Inspector, The, 141
Grimond, Jo, 52, 56, 71–2, 151

Heath, Edward, 28, 39, 47, 52, 56, 62, 70–1, 74, 114
House of Lords, 59, 61, 114, 135, 141, 143, 149, 182

Ideology, 10, 44, 108, 109, 111, 117–18, 121, 129–30, 159, 160, 161, 162, 169, 178
Independent Labour Party, 23
'Iron Law of Oligarchy', 69

Jenkins, Roy, 62

Labour Government: and steel nationalization, 114–17; minority administrations 1924, 1929, 27, 121; of 1964, 3, 98, 111, 119, 121–2
Labour Party: and ideology, 110–17, 129; and pressure-groups, 99; candidate selection, 64–5; Clause IV, 13, 27, 45, 72, 110, 115, 116; Conference, 27, 42; constituency parties, 40–1; disaffiliation of Electrical Trades Union, 188 n.; distribution of power,

Labour Party–*cont.*
73; finance, 75; formation, 8, 23–5; headquarters, 44; National Executive, 26, 41–2, 140; 1960 Conference, 9, 32, 98; 1966 manifesto, 48–9, 111–12; organization, 36; pact with Liberals, 1903, 24; parliamentary party, 32, 38, 39; policies, 60, 119–20, 121–2, 139, 140; revised constitution, 1918, 26
Liberal Party: and ideology, 110; Assembly, 1964, 32; as source of unorthodox policies, 185; decline of fortunes, 13–14; electoral prospects, 8; finance, 75–7; method of electing Leader, 70–2; National Liberal Federation, 22; Newcastle Programme, 1891, 23; 1966 manifesto, 46–7; organization, 38; pact with Labour Party, 1903, 24; policies, 49, 60, 98, 118–19; revival in 1960s, 28; victory at Orpington, 3
Local elections, 3, 31

MacDonald, Ramsay, 27
Macleod, Ian, 43, 55, 62
Macmillan, Harold, 3, 11, 28, 38, 40, 52, 53, 56, 70, 132
Mandate, 2, 30, 123
Maud Commission on Local Government Reform, 80
Maudling, Reginald, 62, 70
Members of Parliament: and public interest, 107; payment of, 26, 55; powers, 6–7; pressure-groups and interests, 100–2, 121, 137; private Members' Bills, 102, 113, 141; selection of candidates to become Members of Parliament, 63–6; social characteristics, 5, 62
Member states, blocs of in UNO, 166–7
Military and politics, 10, 155
Monday Club, the, 9, 181
Must Labour Lose? 45

Nationalist parties, 8
Nuclear disarmament, 34, 45, 99

One-party systems, 33, 170
Opinion polls, 2, 124–5, 183, 189

Parliament: as target for group activity, 101–2; business of, 4
Party agents, 20, 43–4
Party leaders: and groups, 100; as interpreters of ideology, 110–11; characteristics and qualities, 52–4, 62–3; election of, 11 n., 69–72; power of, 72–3; selection process, 63–6
Party of the Crown, the, 17
Pickwick Papers, The, 19–20
Political clubs, 17, 21, 35
Political parties: and consensus, 181–5; and constraints, 133–52; and democracy, 190–3; and local government, 33; and society, 187–90; Burke's definition of, 17; decision-making procedures, 74; distribution of power in, 72–4; election campaigning, 123; evolution, 14–18; finance, 18, 21, 27, 42, 74–6; headquarters, 32, 42, 63–4, 65; in other political systems, ch. 8 *passim*;

Political Parties–*cont.*
leadership, 38, 50–66; operating efficiency, 44–5; patronage, 29–30; programmes, 46–9; purposes, functions, 7–8, ch. 2 *passim*, 109, 149, 161–4, 184–5; slogans, 145; supporters, 66–8; target for pressure-groups, 98–100 (*see also* Conservative Party; Labour Party; Liberal Party)
Political system: as concept, 132–4; as source of constraints on groups, 140–5; types of, 153–4
Powell, Enoch, 62, 71, 120, 181
Pressure for Economic and Social Toryism ('PEST'), 9
Pressure-groups: and balance of interests, 106–7; and consensus, 183–5; and constraints, 133–52; history of, 81–9; in other political systems, ch. 8 *passim*; organizational structure, 105–6, 128; purposes, functions, 7–8, ch. 5 *passim*, 109, 149, 161–4, 184–5; targets of activity, 96–105
Prime Minister: and opinion polls, 124; and policy, 185; conditions of work, 56–7; powers, 11; status of, 57–8
Public opinion, 97, 122, 124, 151

Referendum, 2, 122, 125–6, 178
Reform Act, 1832, 4, 19, 126–7
Reform Act, 1867, 21, 22
Regional government, 31
Representation, 58–63, 162–4 (*see also* Functional representation)
Resale Price Maintenance, 32, 113–14, 115, 122

Rhodesia, 2, 32, 33, 90, 99, 107, 110, 122, 123, 132, 135, 136

Shadow Cabinet, 21, 32
Social class and politics, 10, 23, 34
Social Democratic Federation, 23
Stansted airport proposals, 60, 81, 91, 124
Steel nationalization, 2, 34, 97, 114–17, 123, 162, 182

Taff Vale decision, 24
Thorpe, Jeremy, 52, 56, 63, 71–2
Totalitarian systems, 10, 129, 159
Trades unions: and decision procedures, 140; and Labour Party, 72, 75; candidate sponsorship, 65; political levy, 75–6
Trades Union Congress (TUC): and General Strike, 1926, 87; and white-collar unions, 127–8; change of role, 152; evidence to commissions, 80–1; first meeting, 1868, 83; resolution of 1899 and formation of Labour Party, 8, 24, 99
Transport: interests involved in, 79–80, 88, 94; railway interest in nineteenth century, 84–5; range of interests, 106

United Nations Organization (UNO), 166–7
United States of America: and Constitution, 192; and party ideology, 118; and political developments, 186; Congress, 40; election of 1960, 2;

United States of America–*cont.*
electoral system, 10–11, 64; in UNO, 167; Kennedy, John F., 3, 54, 74; Kennedy, Robert, 50; McCarthy, Eugene, 151; Nixon, Richard M., 3; political system, 154, 157–8, 165; politics in the South, 166, 174; referendum in, 125; registration of lobbyists, 187; Senate, 165

Viet-Nam, 2, 79, 107, 123, 150

Wilson, James Harold, 11, 38, 45, 52, 62, 70, 72, 73, 76, 100, 119, 132, 149, 182 n.
Wyatt, Woodrow, 115–16, 120

WITHDRAWN
St. Scholastica Library
Duluth, Minnesota 55811